# MODERN
# MACRAMÉ

# MODERN MACRAMÉ

## 33 STYLISH PROJECTS FOR YOUR HANDMADE HOME

**EMILY KATZ**
with Johanna Kunin

**PHOTOGRAPHS BY**
Nicole Franzen and Shannon Wolf

1❶
TEN SPEED PRESS
California | New York

# CONTENTS

# INTRODUCTION

I learned macramé from my mom.

At sixteen, my mom made macramé plant hangers by hand-knotting cords of brown jute. She sold her creations at a hair salon, frequented by her mother, so that she could buy her first Martin guitar. The fashion trend then was all about hand-knotted beaded belts and ponchos—anything that swung when you wore it. While sifting through photo albums, I discovered that her childhood home was full of macramé. Plants hung in the windows suspended from beaded macramé plant hangers, and knotted owls watched over the family from the wood-paneled walls of the den.

My parents split up when I was nine years old, and my mom moved across the country. We didn't have much of a relationship while I was growing up; but after turning thirty, I felt like it was time to reconnect. So in 2013, when my boyfriend suggested we visit her while on a trip to the East Coast, I agreed with some trepidation. I didn't know what I would say to her. Would we get along? We barely knew each other. But I did know the story about my mom making macramé.

My home in Portland has plants on nearly every surface—more than a hundred of them. Before the trip to see my mom, I had collected a few vintage macramé plant hangers to display my plants in, but I wanted to learn how to make my own. If my mom could teach me how to macramé, my hope was that we could connect over a common interest.

Before settling into my mother's cozy Connecticut home, we gathered the materials we needed for our afternoon project: cotton cord, a metal ring, and some old beads scavenged from her craft drawer. We stood in her kitchen making plant hangers while my half-sisters baked vegan cookies and my boyfriend sat on the floor serenading us with my mom's Martin guitar—the same one that she'd bought so many years ago with her earnings from making macramé.

It was a sweet and beautiful moment, one that is forever etched into my memory. After the trip, my boyfriend and I hung the plant hangers in our guest bathroom, and I mostly forgot about macramé. I made a few pieces as gifts for friends, but besides that, I was busy doing other things. During that period, I was working as an art director for a local company and didn't make a lot of time for crafting.

That fall, a Japanese magazine called *Liniere* was in Portland doing a feature on DIY interiors and design. They had discovered our home through my Instagram account and wanted to feature us. Their team wandered around our house, snapping photos and asking through a translator about special details we had created in our space. How did you make the countertops? What inspired the hand-screen-printed toe kicks for the stairs? Why do you have a mirror over your stove? One woman, Kanae Ishii, renowned for her *Love Customizer* craft and DIY books in Japan, asked me where the macramé plant hangers that hung in our bathroom came from.

I began to tell her the story of reconnecting with my mom and how meaningful it was. She listened to the translator and then asked, "But where do we get them?"

At this time, macramé had only recently resurfaced and wasn't as readily available as it is now. I didn't know where to send them to find it, so I suggested they check out the flea market or local thrift shops in hopes of finding some fun vintage pieces. After they left, I thought, "What if I taught them myself?" and called to see if they had any time to come back and learn how to make a macramé plant hanger. Early the next day they arrived back at my home, and I taught my very first macramé workshop to Japanese magazine editors in my living room.

Since then, I've gone on to macramé area rugs, ceiling installations, daybeds, head-boards, tents, and wedding backdrops. I even fashioned a skeleton costume for Halloween out of macramé. I have taught macramé workshops in Los Angeles, New York, London, Copenhagen, and throughout Japan. I've grown to appreciate the fact that macramé's threads run deep through history, from Bedouin caravans to European courts, and from turn-of-the-century sailors' hammocks to fine Victorian handicrafts. But I am especially delighted to contribute to its modern renaissance, and am grateful that this medium has inspired a reconnection with my mother that I hadn't imagined possible.

Nowadays, you can find modern macramé everywhere. It's the creatively homespun bag on the shoulder of that boho-chic model or your stylish best friend. It holds the plant hanging in the background of that Instagram shot, the fiber art on the wall of a cutting-edge art gallery or boutique hotel. It's also the textured headboard, the elegant hanging lamp, and the gorgeous patio garlands in this book.

There's a reason macramé has resurfaced. More and more of us are seeking a bit of warmth, craft, and adornment in the midst of modern life. And macramé—in its clean-yet-dreamy, updated incarnation—is a perfect point of entry into creating a unique, one-of-a-kind, handmade lifestyle, one that is literally at your fingertips.

If you have ever wanted to learn macramé but didn't know where to begin, or even if you are a seasoned knot tier, this book will provide both inspiration and detailed instruction to help guide you on your journey of this beautiful craft.

# MACRAMÉ BASICS

# INCORPORATING MACRAMÉ INTO YOUR HOME

From a glamorous and art-filled Spanish-style home in Los Angeles to a bohemian loft in Copenhagen to a handcrafted cabin in upstate New York, the homes featured in this book all share one thing in common: modern macramé.

Whether you live in a cozy apartment, a sprawling ranch-style, or a Brooklyn brownstone, there is a modern way to bring macramé into your home, and these pages will show you how. Clear, concise how-to photography and easy-to-follow instructions guide you through the thirty-three projects featured, while the lush interior photographs inspire you to style them into your own space. Whether a standout lampshade as a textural focal point beside a sofa in a brightly painted living room, a headboard adding a sophisticated touch above a luxurious bed, or even the subtle knotting on a broom handle, these patterns range from the understated to the bold.

Each project is photographed at least two times, in two different settings in order to illustrate the variety of ways you might incorporate them into your home: The Circle Game Plant Hanger (page 58) hangs just as beautifully in a penny-tiled bathroom beneath a skylight as it does in a minimal and refined guest house with architectural plants and midcentury furnishings. The Sisters of the Moon Wall Hanging (page 105) is perfect as a door curtain to conceal a bedroom in a minimal loft, as a shower curtain in a cute bathroom, or as a statement piece in a home with a modernist vibe.

Whether your style is minimal, midcentury, boho, or Scandinavian-inspired, there is a perfect project here for you to truly craft your handmade home.

Above: The Gold Dust Woman Wall Hanging (page 85) adds the perfect texture to a monochrome galley wall.

Far Left: The stylish Pillow Cover (page 227) looks chic on a structural sofa.

Left: A pretty bouquet arranged in the Hanging Basket (page 67) pairs playfully with a speckled ceramic vase.

# THE HISTORY OF MACRAMÉ

When people ask me what I do for a living, I tell them, "I make macramé installations and teach workshops around the world." More often than not they say, "Huh? What is macramé?" The question gives me such pleasure. It means that I have a lot more work to do in sharing my appreciation for the craft.

Thought to have originated on the Arabian Peninsula in the thirteenth century, the word for *macramé* in Arabic, *migramah,* translates to "fringe." I picture the weavers of the time, finely knotting harnesses for camels to keep the flies and sand out of the animals' eyes—and creating something beautiful at the same time, form and function together.

In Turkish, the word *makrama* means "to napkin" or "to towel" and refers to the method of twisting and knotting the edges of handwoven fabrics in order to secure them—as seen on Turkish towels.

Knotting has even earlier origins. Fringe and hand-knotted details adorned costumes and celebration garb from Babylon to Assyria. Macramé was showing up in Chinese folk art from the Tang (618–907) and Song (960–1279) dynasties. The familiar knot work, imbued with fable, was used to decorate halls and palaces. Chinese royalty decorated everything, from dresses, mirrors, pouches, and fans to furniture, with exquisite knots.

In the early twelfth century, the Moors brought macramé to Spain, and it spread into Europe through trade and war. But there were other ways macramé made its way across the globe. Sailors, in the golden age of sailing, from the fifteenth to nineteenth centuries, helped spread the functional practice throughout the world. During the long months at sea, with rope and time at their disposal, they made macramé objects with which to barter when stopping at various ports. They also used macramé to decorate the ships as well as make their own gear: hammocks, belts, and bell fringes.

Macramé eventually made its way to England in the seventeenth century in the court of Queen Mary, where it was used for altar cloths and vestments. The royal court took pleasure in being at the top of fashion trends and obsessively integrated new lace and knotting techniques into their garments.

When I was seventeen, my family lived in Italy for six months. I was wildly independent and spent many weekends traveling around by myself. I took the train to Verona, where I taught a gaggle of ladies how to crochet while we drank decadently rich hot chocolate. Unbeknownst to me at the time, I was dipping my toes into teaching craft.

On that same trip, I visited Venice and took the ferry to Burano, a tiny island known for hundreds of years of lace making. The custom still holds strong today; if you visit Burano, you'll see beautifully wrinkled, smiling women tatting away at their intricately detailed laces. Many of which are made with silk and a hook, but some are hand-knotted as well.

While traveling through Japan in April 2016, I visited the home of a famous ceramic artist who had a beautiful collection of antiques from around the world. In one of the glass cases, I saw a selection of intricately macraméd vests, dyed with indigo and other natural pigments. I was told they were ceremonial dress from the eighteenth century, to be worn by a man over his kimono during a wedding or celebration. The Japanese knotting may be called *hanamusubi* but it is still macramé to me.

In the United States, macramé was taught in schools in the 1960s and became a popular craft. It seemed like all of my friends had a parent who made macramé in their youth. Fashioned into lampshades, plant hangers, belts, necklaces, clothing, wall hangings, and, of course, owls, macramé filled the homes of the 1960s and '70s with its rustic hippie vibe. Hundreds of patterns were sold in the form of thin magazine-size pamphlets, full of plant-hanger designs and ideas to make almost anything out of macramé. I do believe that there was a time in the 1970s when nearly every house in America had at least one macramé plant hanger somewhere. I remember finding photos of my grandmother's house from that era showing a room filled with hanging plants. Visiting her home again last year, I saw she still has some of them, dappling the light in her kitchen.

The craft died out in the 1980s, but everything old is new again. Macramé has returned in fashion and home design with the resurgence of love for all things 1970s. From high-end fashion houses such as Christian Dior and Salvatore Ferragamo to Chanel and Dolce & Gabbana, macramé has graced runways and haute couture, is now available at large retailers such as Free People and Anthropologie (where my own plant hangers can be found), and is sold by many makers on Etsy and on their own sites.

I am grateful to have found my own place in the history of macramé, sharing with the world the craft that reconnected me to my mom, and adding a new milestone in macramé's long story.

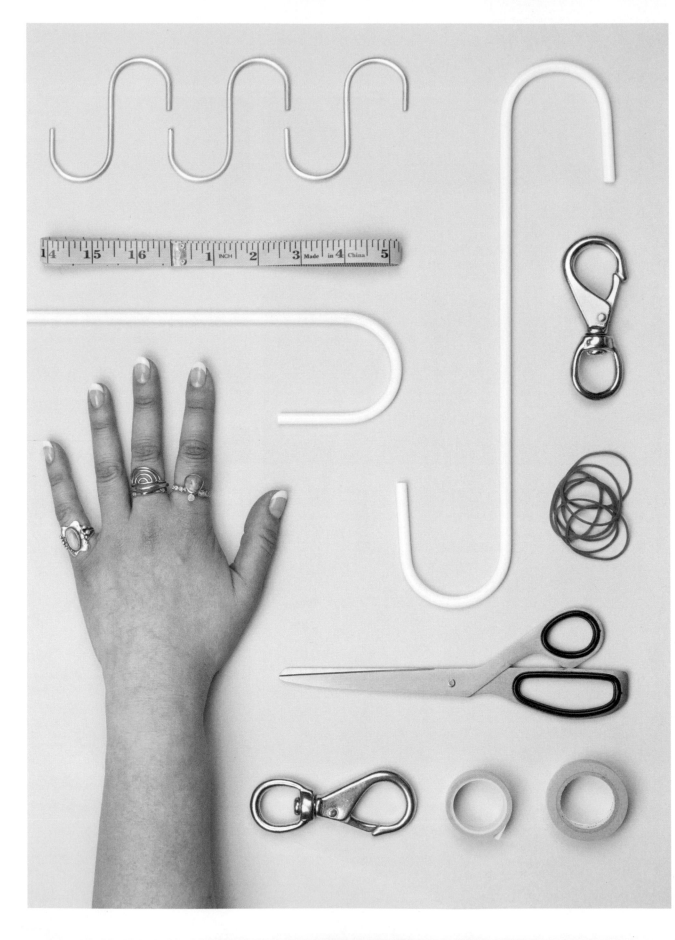

# GETTING STARTED

You are ready to learn macramé! But where do you start?

First, you'll want to choose a project that fits your skill level. Each pattern in this book has a difficulty rating:

**Beginner +**

• Start here if you are new to macramé. These projects are the quickest and simplest to make.

**Intermediate ++**

• Once you've gotten your feet wet and are game for a little more complexity, try your hand at one of these.

**Advanced/Adventurous +++**

• These projects are complicated and/or large in scale. Executing them successfully takes the kind of finesse that one gains through hands-on experience—plus a healthy dose of patience—but all that hard work makes the end result particularly rewarding.

Once you've chosen a project, just a few short steps remain between you and your macramé creation: gathering the right tools and materials together, setting up your workspace, and learning the basic knots. This chapter will get you ready to mount the first rope of your project.

## TOOLS

You don't need many tools to make macramé. Most of the time, your hands, rope, sharp scissors, and a measuring tape are all it takes; although for some projects in this book, you'll need additional everyday items like masking tape or rubber bands; and a few more require special hardware. If you're stumped on where to find something, see Resources (page 240) for a list of suppliers.

Before you begin, carefully read over the pattern and gather everything you'll need to complete it. While I work, I like to keep things I'll be reaching for repeatedly in the large front pocket of a smock.

## MAKING SPACE

Macramé transforms rope into an array of forms, but not all sizes and shapes can be made with the same setup. Before you can get knotting, you'll need to configure a comfortable workspace that both inspires you and accommodates the particular shape you would like to create.

You don't need anything fancy to make macramé, but I like the idea of setting intention and time for your crafting. Make sure the light is bright enough to see what you are doing, and put on some music that gets you in the groove. For most hanging pieces, I start working standing up and then move to a chair or even the floor as the piece grows longer. Some projects in this book can be held in your hands or hung over a dowel while you work. Others are easiest to work when secured to a corkboard or other flat surface.

Having the tools you will need nearby, including chairs or stools of different heights and a floor cushion or two, can make or break your knotting session. *Remember that your hands are your most important tools.* Support them and avoid injury by keeping your back and shoulders comfortable and taking frequent breaks.

Over the years, my macramé business has grown into a team of women, knotting away in a spacious studio with twelve-foot ceilings and lots of natural light. But when I started, it was just me making macramé in a tiny spare room. Don't feel like you have to have the perfect space in order to begin. You can create beautiful art wherever you are.

### Horizontal Setup

Some pieces are best worked across a flat surface. When making such pieces, the trick is to keep tension on the filler cord(s) while creating space under the knotting in which to maneuver the working cords. I usually accomplish this by tying or clamping the top of my work to something stationary. Once I start knotting, I place a pillow or book beneath the knots worked most recently to elevate them.

**Corkboard and Pins** Small projects made with finer rope, string, or yarn can be secured to a corkboard or a piece of sturdy cardboard using pins.

**C-Clamp** Hook longer projects made with heavier rope onto a C-clamp attached to a work table or countertop. If desired, place wood or cardboard scraps between the clamp edges and the table itself to avoid damaging the table. If you need your piece to rotate freely while you work, attach it to the hook with a swivel clip. This is especially helpful when working long, spiraling columns of knots.

### Vertical Setup

Many projects are best worked in a hanging position, using dowels and/or hooks. Hang your work at least a foot higher than the finished length listed in the pattern whenever possible. This will allow you to finish your project comfortably.

**Supported Dowel** Clothing racks laden with tools, cut ropes, and works in progress are a constant in my studio. They're a great place to keep everything organized and hang many kinds of projects while you work on them. If your space is limited, however, a well-secured curtain, shower, or closet rod can work just as well.

**Hanging Dowel** A dowel can also be hung from the ceiling using hooks and scraps of rope. To do this, first install two hooks in the ceiling several inches closer together than the length of the dowel. Then, measure how far below the hooks you would like the dowel to hang. Tie the ends of a piece of scrap rope together securely to form a loop that roughly matches this measurement when pulled taut. Repeat with a second piece of rope to form a second loop. Place one loop over each hook, and then bring the dowel through both loops so that it hangs horizontally. If you'd like to raise your work as it grows longer, simply retie the loops and make them smaller, or set the dowel directly on the hooks.

**Hook** For shorter projects, loop an S-hook over a clothing rack or closet rod. For longer ones, a hook in the ceiling may work better. Here again, the height can be adjusted by using scrap rope, and if your project is worked in the round (i.e., is tubular in shape), the addition of a swivel clip will allow your project to rotate freely as you work on it.

## Unexpected Spaces

I've given you a few setup ideas here, but feel free to branch out. Once you start looking for potential macramé-making locations, you might just find them all around you! Chairs, doorknobs, coatracks, bed frames, ladders, clipboards, canvas stretchers, and more can all be used with a little ingenuity. If you're fortunate enough to find yourself with beautiful weather and enough time to craft, you could even head outside and hang your work between sturdy trees or beneath an arbor—who knows what dreamy space you might discover!

IMPORTANT SAFETY NOTE: Always take care when hanging anything, especially from the ceiling. Only utilize hardware that is designed for use in your wall or ceiling material and that is made to accommodate at least twice the weight of the rope and hardware used in your project. If you have any concerns, ask for help at your local hardware store.

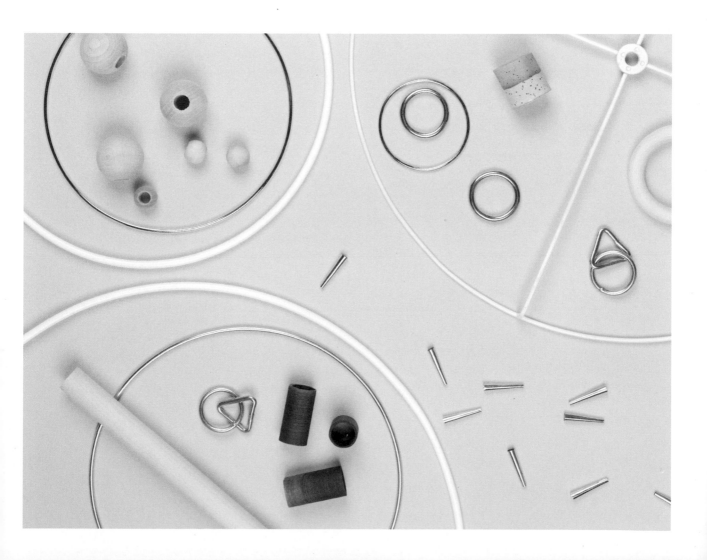

## AN ARRAY OF KNOTTING MATERIALS

Cotton, jute, hemp, jersey, and wool; braided and twisted; cord, rope, and twine—in macramé, your potential palette is nearly limitless, with varying weights, textures, and colors to suit any style and purpose you can dream up.

Natural-colored cotton rope is the mainstay of modern macramé. It is fresh, bright, easy on the hands, and looks fantastic in nearly every kind of home. In this book, we expand beyond cotton and introduce other amazing materials, from the giant felted wool yarn of the Many Diamonds Rug (page 178) to the fine and drapey hemp rope used to make a set of Ghost Ranch Place Mats (page 202) to the sturdy, plied polypropylene of the Basket (page 235), which is tough enough even for the outdoors. The best way to get to know the personality of each material is to work with it; however, some basic knowledge beforehand will give you a head start. Here's an introduction to the four types of rope used in this book.

### Plied

Like the cotton rope I reach for most often, the majority of the ropes used in this book are plied. Plied ropes are made by twisting multiple strands of material together. The plies can be unraveled to produce beautiful fringe at the edge of the macramé piece; however, plied ropes may unravel a bit on their own as you work. To avoid this, wrap the ends with tape until your project is finished. This usually won't be necessary, but some rope has a looser ply than others and naturally wants to untwist.

### Braided

Unintended unraveling isn't a problem for braided ropes, like the ½-inch braided cotton rope used in the Geological Shift Wall Hanging (page 94). In fact, ropes constructed this way can't easily be unwoven for effect like those that are plied. They are, however, particularly strong and durable.

### Felted

The wool yarn used in the Many Diamonds Rug (page 178) is felted together, and if you have ever shrunk your favorite sweater in the washer, you've seen just how powerful felting can be! Used intentionally, felting can produce amazing things, like this unique, handmade yarn. You can also use felting at home to quickly and seamlessly join two woolen yarn ends together. Simply tease the fibers apart a bit along the first few inches of both ends and wet them. Overlap the teased-out ends and rub them together quickly between your palms until the connection is strong. This process is known as *spit-splicing*.

### Knit

The yarn used to make the Beaded Plant Hanger (page 55) is actually made out of knitted fabric, which gives it some serious stretch! Check out that pattern for some tips on how to work with this material.

### Making Substitutions

I really enjoy experimenting with different materials and encourage you to do the same if you are so inspired! But before you dive in and start cutting, please note that even small differences in rope diameter and properties can change how much length you will need. If you substitute rope with a larger diameter, for instance, you will need more than the pattern states. If your rope is stretchier or squishier, you may not need as much. I strongly recommend saving yourself the headache (and heartache) of running out of rope in the middle of a project by making a swatch. For a how-to, see How Long Should the Ropes Be? (page 34).

# KNOTS AND TECHNIQUES

When I began making macramé, I knew how to make only two knots: the Square and the Half Square. To this day, these are often the only knots I use when designing. Over time, of course, I have incorporated more knots into my work, and although those first two retain their starring roles, several others make frequent cameo appearances.

You'll find instructions for every knot in this book on the following pages, but don't feel like you have to learn them all at once. Each pattern lists the specific knots you need to complete the project. If you prefer to learn as you go, you can add knots to your repertoire as you need them.

## ROPES AND CORDS: A NOTE ON TERMINOLOGY

In addition to their everyday meanings, the terms "rope" and "cord" each have a second definition in this book that is specific to macramé. The term "rope" is used to refer to an entire cut length of *any* knotting material, be it yarn, string, twine, or, naturally, rope. A "cord," on the other hand, is either side of a "rope" that has been folded in half and mounted or otherwise made ready for knotting. This means that a single "rope," once folded, yields two "cords," with or around which knotting can be formed. In other words, "ropes" are the lengths that you cut at the beginning of your project. "Cords" are what you knot with.

Tip: I always recommend buying 10 percent more rope than a pattern calls for to be sure you won't run out of materials. With colored rope this is especially important, as dye lots may differ.

## BEGINNINGS

Incorporating a new rope into a project is called *mounting*. The first step in most projects is to mount rope(s) onto a dowel or piece of hardware, like a ring; although rope(s) may also be mounted onto other rope(s) or onto existing knotting as well. The easiest and most common way to do this is the Lark's Head Knot (LHK) or its opposite, the Reverse Lark's Head Knot (RLHK).

### Lark's Head Knot (LHK)

1 Make a loop at the center of the rope, and bring it in front of the dowel. [A]

2 Fold the loop back around the dowel. [B]

3 Pull the ends of the rope down through the loop. [C]

4 Make sure the rope is divided precisely in half and then tighten the knot. [D]

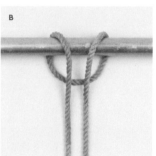
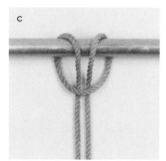
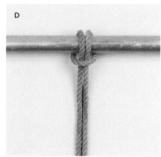

### Reverse Lark's Head Knot (RLHK)

1 Make a loop at the center of the rope, and bring it up behind the dowel. [A]

2 Fold the loop forward over the dowel. [B]

3 Pull the ends of the rope forward through the loop. [C]

4 Make sure the rope is divided precisely in half and then tighten the knot. [D]

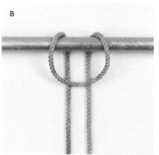
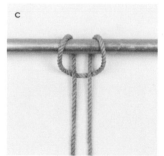
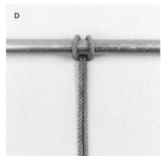

## HALF SQUARES

The classic Half Square Knot (HSK) and its mirror image, the Right Half Square Knot (RHSK), are made by knotting two outer cords, called *working cords*, around two inner cords, called *filler cords*. This basic method is shown here. Occasionally in this book, however, these knots are worked around more than two filler cords or around a rigid object like a ring or dowel. If so, this will be specified in the individual pattern.

### Half Square Knot (HSK)

1 Bring the left working cord (gray) over both filler cords and under the right working cord (white). [A]

2 Bring the right working cord (white) under the filler cords and over the left working cord (gray). [B]

3 Tighten the knot. [C]

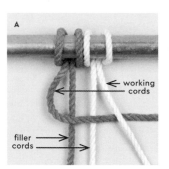

### Right Half Square Knot (RHSK)

1 Bring the right working cord (white) over both filler cords and under the left working cord (gray). [A]

2 Bring the left working cord (gray) under the filler cords and over the right working cord (white). [B]

3 Tighten the knot. [C]

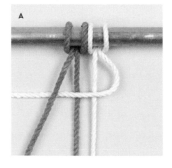

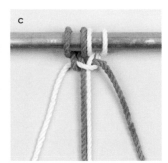

## SQUARES

One of each type of Half Square worked back to back forms a Square. In this book, Squares that begin with a Half Square Knot (HSK) are called Square Knots (SKs), and those that begin with a Right Half Square Knot (RHSK) are called Right-Facing Square Knots (RSKs).

### Square Knot (SK)

1  Work an HSK.

2  Work an RHSK.

3  Tighten the knot.

You've now made one Square Knot (SK). This knot is also known as the Left-Facing Square Knot. In the photo at right top, note the vertical line of white rope on the knot's left side. Throughout this book, I refer to it simply as the Square Knot (SK) because the Right-Facing Square Knot (RSK) is rarely used.

### Right-Facing Square Knot (RSK)

1  Work an RHSK.

2  Work an HSK.

3  Tighten the knot.

You've now made one Right-Facing Square Knot (RSK). In the photo at right bottom, note the vertical line of gray rope on the right side of the knot.

## Mounting with a Half Square Knot (HSK) or Square Knot (SK)

You can also mount one rope onto another, or onto a rigid object like a dowel or ring, using a Half Square Knot (HSK) or Square Knot (SK).

1 Bring the center of the rope behind the object (or mounting cord). [A]

2 Bring the left working cord across the object (or mounting cord) and under the working cord on the right. [B]

3 Bring the right working cord under the object (or mounting cord) and over the working cord on the left. [C]

4 Tighten the knot. If you are mounting with an HSK, stop here. [D] If mounting with an SK, continue with 5 and 6.

5 Work an RHSK around the object (or mounting cord). [E]

6 Tighten to complete the SK. [F]

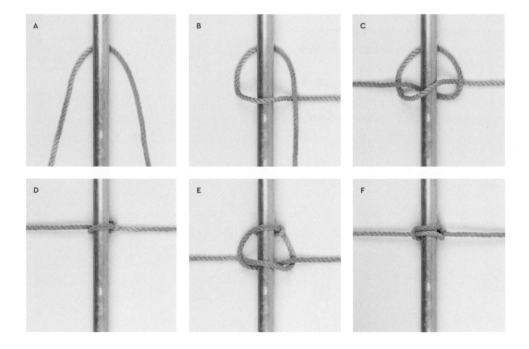

## KNOTS WORKED IN SEQUENCE

Two or more knots worked directly above one another using the same cords are said to be *worked in sequence*. Knots worked in sequence form vertical chains called *columns*. Some of the columns in this book consist of more than one knot type, and some also have varying amounts of space between the knots. Most, however, are of the two types described here: sinnets and spirals. Each of these consists of knots of just one type, worked without any space left between them.

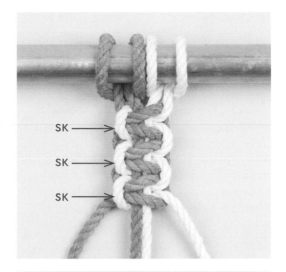

### Sinnet of Square Knots

A *sinnet* is a column of knots of a single type. Sinnets of Square Knots (SKs) are used frequently throughout this book. You can determine the number of SKs in a sinnet by counting the vertical bumps on its left side. The one pictured at right top contains three SKs in all.

### Sinnet of Right-Facing Square Knots

To determine the number of Right-Facing Square Knots (RSKs) in a sinnet, count the vertical bumps on the right side of the knots. The sinnet shown in the right middle photo is made of RSKs.

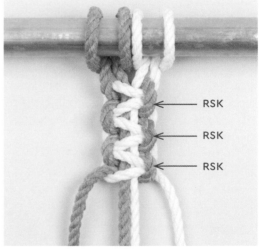

### Half Square Knot Spiral

Half Square Knots (HSKs) worked one after another spiral to the right around the filler cords. Right Half Square Knots (RHSKs) worked one after another spiral to the left. The spiral shown at right bottom is made of HSKs. Note that its shape is a bit like a twisted ladder. You can count the number of knots in a spiral by counting the number of ladder "rungs."

## ALTERNATING KNOTS

An alternating knot is worked between the two knots above it by using half of the cords extending from each of them. Alternating knots produce planes of knotting, called *netting*. The closer together the alternating knots, the denser the netting will be.

### Alternating Square Knots (ASK)

Almost all of the alternating knots in this book are Square Knots (SKs). To work an Alternating Square Knot (ASK), work an SK using the two rightmost cords of the knot on the left and the two leftmost cords of the knot on the right.

The most visually pleasing Alternating Square Knot (ASK) netting has even spacing between the knots. Measure the distance between knots frequently to ensure that it remains consistent. The distance between alternating knots should be measured diagonally, from the edge of one knot to the next. (See Before You Begin, page 37.)

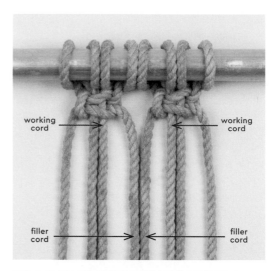

working cord → ← working cord

filler cord → ← filler cord

## ALTERNATING ROWS AND ROUNDS

Patterns consisting of alternating knots are written out as a series of horizontal rows (if the piece is flat, like a wall hanging) or rounds (if tube-shaped, like a lantern or plant hanger). Unless otherwise specified, work each row or round directly below the previous one, and work rows from left to right.

### Alternating Rows of Square Knots

The photo at right top shows three rows of Alternating Square Knots (ASKs). Note that the first and last two cords of the second row are not worked, which leaves a gap along the edge. This is the case for every even-numbered row of ASKs. The instructions for the knotting pictured might be written in a couple of different ways. Most often, they would simply read, "Work 3 rows of ASKs." If written out row by row, however, they would look like this.

Row 1: Work 2 SKs.

Row 2: Skip 2 cords, work an SK, then skip 2 cords.

Row 3: Repeat Row 1.

### Alternating Rounds of Square Knots

When working alternating knots in the round, you work every cord in each round. The photo at right middle shows 3 rounds of ASKs with ¾" of space left between the knots. The instructions for this knotting pattern would read, "Work 3 rounds of ASKs, ¾" apart."

### Alternating Rows/Rounds of Two (or More) Square Knots

More lengthy and/or complex rows can be alternated to produce netting as well. One such pattern used frequently in this book is shown in the photo at right bottom. Note that each of its rows is made up of sinnets of two Square Knots (SKs).

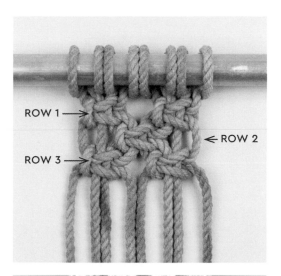

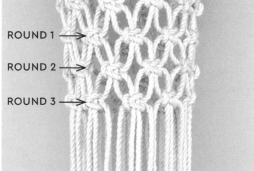

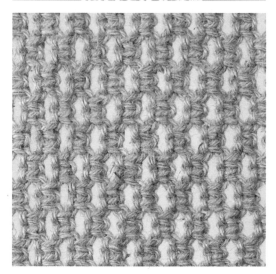

## HITCHES

Three types of hitch knots are used in this book: Horizontal Double Half Hitch (HDHH), Horizontal Triple Half Hitch (HTHH), and Vertical Double Half Hitch (VDHH). Like alternating knots, these knots are worked in horizontal rows or rounds. Unlike alternating knots, the method used to form them is different when a row or round is worked from left to right than when worked from right to left.

### Horizontal Double Half Hitch (HDHH)

Each Horizontal Double Half Hitch (HDHH) knot is made up of two Half Hitch (HH) knots made from the same working cord. A row of HDHH produces a raised bar across your work.

### HDHH Worked Left to Right

1 Make a Half Hitch (HH) by holding the filler cord (white) horizontally in front of the working cords (gray), leaving a tail of several inches, and looping the leftmost working cord up and around the filler cord. Then bring it down behind the filler cord and to the left of itself and tighten. [A]

2 Work a second HH with the same working cord, looping it around the filler cord to the right of the first loop. [B]

3 Tighten to complete one HDHH. [C]

4 To complete a row of HDHHs, repeat steps 1–3 with the next cord to the right, and so on to the end of the row. [D]

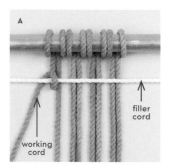

working cord
filler cord

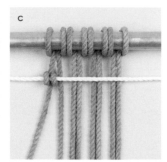

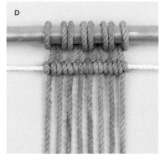

### HDHH Worked Right to Left

1 Loop the rightmost working cord up and around the filler cord and to the right of itself and tighten. [A]

2 Work another HH to the left of the first and tighten. You've now completed one HDHH. [B]

3 To complete the row, repeat steps 1–2 across the remaining working cords. [C]

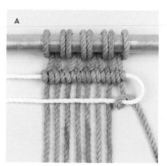

### Mounting with an HDHH

You can also use a Horizontal Double Half Hitch (HDHH) to mount a new rope onto an existing filler cord. Use the following instructions to mount a new cord within a row of HDHH worked from left to right. This method also works if you are working from right to left. In that case, just work the HDHH in the opposite direction (as in HDHH Worked Right to Left, above).

1 Hold the center of the new rope (gray) behind the filler cord (white), bringing one end up and out of the way and allowing the other to hang down vertically. [A]

2 Loop the lower end of the new rope around the mounting cord and to the left of itself. Tighten. [B]

3 Work an HH to the right of the first loop. [C]

4 Bring the two new cords together and adjust the knot so that they are equal in length. Tighten. [D]

## Horizontal Triple Half Hitch (HTHH)

A Horizontal Triple Half Hitch (HTHH) is formed by making three Half Hitch (HH) knots in a row with a single working cord.

## Vertical Double Half Hitch (VDHH)

When making Vertical Double Half Hitch knots (VDHHs), you use a single working cord to form Double Half Hitch knots across multiple filler cords. Like the HDHH, each VDHH consists of two HHs.

### VDHH Worked Left to Right

1 Work an HH around the leftmost filler cord (gray) by bringing the working cord (white) behind and around the filler cord and then over itself. [A]

2 Tighten and, once more, bring the working cord around the filler cord and back over itself, forming a second HH below the first. [B]

3 Tighten. You've now completed one VDHH. [C]

4 Repeat across the remaining filler cords to complete the row. [D]

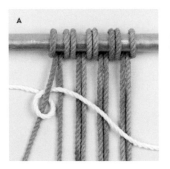
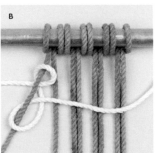
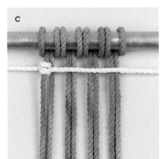
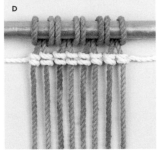

### VDHH Worked Right to Left

1 Work an HH by bringing the working cord behind and around the rightmost filler cord and then over itself.

2 Tighten and, once more, bring the working cord around the filler cord and over itself. [A]

3 Tighten to complete one VDHH. [B]

4 Repeat across the remaining filler cords to complete the row. [C]

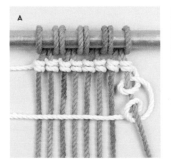

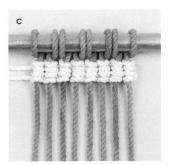

## ODDS AND ENDINGS

Just one more knot and two time-saving techniques and you're on your way.

### Overhand Knot (OK)

The most basic of knots, the Overhand Knot (OK) requires just one cord and is made by wrapping one end of the cord around the other and then tightening.

### Bundling

Very long ropes are difficult to work with and have a tendency to become hopelessly tangled piles of spaghetti unless they are bundled up ahead of time.

1 Fold the rope in half and mark the center with a piece of tape.

2 Starting from one end, make a bundle by folding the rope every 8 to 12 inches. Stop 3 to 4 feet from the center, and secure the bundle with a rubber band.

3 Repeat step 2 on the other side. When working with the bundled rope, simply hold the rubber band in place while pulling rope from the bundle when you need more length.

### Beading

Usually, incorporating a bead into knotwork is as simple as sliding it into place and knotting below it. Sometimes, however, this process is hampered by frayed ends or the need to fit a bead with a small hole around more than one rope. In either case, simply do the following.

1 Tape the ends of the rope(s) together.

2 Slide the bead into place.

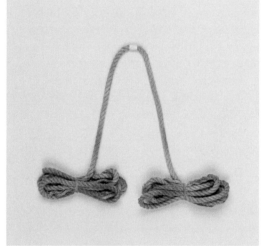

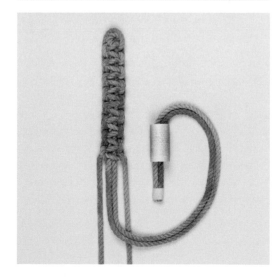

# HOW LONG SHOULD THE ROPES BE?

An age-old macramé dilemma: You don't want to end up with piles of excess rope when your piece is finished, but you *really* don't want to run out of rope a few knots shy of completion. If you make enough macramé, you'll likely encounter one or both of these situations. Although neither is the end of the world, it's best to do whatever you can to prevent them.

If you're making a project in this book using the suggested material, you can set this question aside for now and simply use the lengths listed in the pattern. But what if you want to make alterations to a pattern or use a different material? What if you decide to design something yourself? Then you'll want to make some calculations before you start cutting.

Above all, the common wisdom is to err on the side of too much length rather than too little. This is because, while no one wants to end up with piles of excess trimmings, most scraps can be salvaged and reused. Coming up short, on the other hand, can be a difficult problem to solve, potentially creating a blemish in your knotwork.

Handmade craft is not a science, and we are not machines. Try as we might to achieve perfect uniformity, every knot we make will vary from its neighbors just a little bit. On top of that, we all use our hands a little differently. Some of us tend to work more tightly, others on the looser side. And unless we are the most seasoned of artisans, the knots we make today might not look exactly like those from yesterday or tomorrow. In one sense, this subtle variation is an asset, enriching what we make with handmade character and unique personality; however, when it comes to reliably calculating how long to cut ropes for macramé, human imperfections produce a practical challenge. Just how much rope should we allow for each knot, if they are all slightly different? Fortunately, it is possible to boil all of this complication down to solid numbers.

## SWATCHING

If you are changing the material and/or size of a project with just one repeated knot or pattern, swatching is a great place to start. A *swatch* is a small sample of knotted material that can yield a lot of helpful information, including the average length of rope needed to produce a particular amount of knotting.

Let's say, for example, that you want to make a 10-foot-long sinnet of Square Knots with 6 inches of fringe at the bottom but aren't sure how much rope you will need.

1 First, you'll need to cut two equal-size pieces of the rope you'll be using for your project. These can measure anywhere from 36" for finer materials (like the worsted weight hemp string used in the Wrapped Votive, page 209) to 80" or more for thicker rope (like the ½"-diameter braided cotton rope used in the Gold Dust Woman Wall Hanging, page 85). Whatever length you choose, be sure to both *measure* and *remember* that length precisely. Also, keep in mind that the longer your ropes, the bigger your swatch, and

the bigger your swatch, the more accurate an estimate it will yield. In other words, it pays to not be overly skimpy here. For this example, let's make the ropes 64" long.

2  Fold both ropes in half over a dowel or hook.

3  Work a sinnet of Square Knots until your working cords become too short to knot any further.

4  Measure the length of the sinnet as precisely as possible. Do not include any unknotted rope in this measurement.

5  Divide the length of the rope you started with (before folding it or making any knots) by the length of the sinnet. This tells you how much rope you used, on average, to make 1" of knotting. Let's say your 64"-long ropes worked up into an 8"-long sinnet. Since 64 ÷ 8 = 8, it took you an average of 8" of rope to make 1" of sinnet.

6  Multiply this number by your desired length. That's 8 × 10' = 80' of rope to make the 10' sinnet in our example.

7  Don't forget the fringe! You'll need to multiply your desired fringe length by two, since each rope will be folded in half. In our example, you wanted 6" (0.5') of fringe at the bottom. You would double that and add it in, for a total of 81' of length needed for each rope.

8  This estimate is a good starting point, but I always recommend adding 10 percent to be safe. In our example, that would bring the grand total to about 89'.

This is just one example. You can make a swatch of any repetitive knotting pattern, including those made with alternating knots and Vertical or Horizontal Double Half Hitches; however, for patterns made from rows or rounds of knots rather than a single column, you will first need to determine how many ropes are needed to accurately represent your pattern before completing the previous steps. For example, to make a swatch of ASKs, at minimum you would need four ropes to make a swatch, or enough to produce two SKs in a row.

## ESTIMATING BASED ON KNOT DENSITY

Swatching is very reliable, but only if your project has a single overall knotting pattern. If you're making something more complex (i.e., with multiple/nonrepetitive knotting patterns or some areas that are more densely knotted than others), here is a quicker, albeit rougher, method of estimation.

1  For areas in which the knots will be more than 1" apart, multiply the desired finished length of that area by 6; or for areas in which the knots will be less than 1" apart, multiply the desired finished length of that area by 8.

2  Add the rope length estimates for each part of your project together and then add 10 percent.

3  Add twice the desired length of any fringe.

If additional ropes will be added in the middle of your project, be sure to take this into account when calculating. Also, note that the thicker your material, the more you will need. If the rope you are working with has a diameter of ½" or larger, you may want to add another 10 to 20 percent. If your rope's diameter is smaller than ⅛" (3mm), you may be able to get by with less.

# BEFORE YOU BEGIN

These guidelines will apply to all of the patterns in this book.

• Fold all ropes precisely in half before mounting unless otherwise stated. Take a moment to make sure the ends are still even in length after mounting.

• Square Knots (SKs) and Half Square Knots (HSKs) are left-facing except where noted.

• To determine the distance between rows or rounds, measure the length of the unknotted rope between the edge of one knot and the next. Do not measure from the center of the knots.

   - Between rows worked in sequence, the rope measured hangs vertically. [A]

   - Between alternating rows, the rope extends diagonally. [B]

• When specifying the distance between a new row/round/knot and the one above it, the pattern will simply say to work the new row/round/knot *x" below*. For example, an instruction stating, *2" below, work a row of SKs*, would mean "Work a row of square knots 2 inches below the previous one."

• If a distance below is not specified, do not leave any space between rows/rounds/knots.

• Abbreviations for knot names are used throughout the book. Each pattern lists the knots you'll need to complete it, along with their abbreviations.

• When in doubt, refer to Knots and Techniques (page 22) and the Glossary (page 241) for further clarification.

If you find yourself getting discouraged, instead of giving up, let your creativity flow. The most important thing to remember? Have fun!

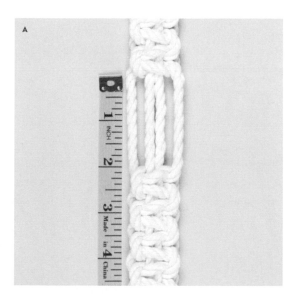

# PLANT HANGERS

Let's begin with that classic crafter's gateway drug, the plant hanger. Its casual, effortless style enhances the look of most spaces, and elevates even the smallest and most ordinary houseplant; both literally and figuratively. Given how quick and easy plant hangers are to knot, it's no wonder they have led many minimalists to transform their flora-starved homes into urban jungles.

PLANT HANGERS

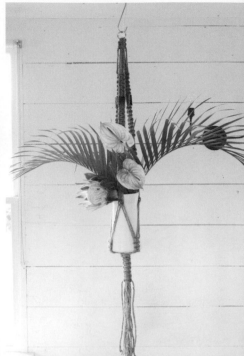

Of course, your plant-hanger styling options don't begin and end with houseplants. Try nesting a rattan basket or copper bowl filled with fruits or vegetables inside. Arrange several hangers to contain a floating herb garden. Or let the Beaded Plant Hanger add elegance and sophistication to a tropical floral arrangement. The ideas are endless.

## PLANT HANGER POINTERS

• When making plant hangers, always measure carefully so that your knots line up properly. That way your finished piece (and its contents) will be properly balanced.

• When you get to the bottom, feel free to make additional knotting or leave the fringe a bit longer than the pattern states, if desired. Make your plant hanger to suit both you and your space.

• In each pattern, you will find a measurement for the finished length of the plant hanger when empty. Once you place a pot inside, however, the plant hanger's total length may actually *decrease* by several inches. This is because the ropes of the plant hanger no longer hang down vertically with a pot inside, but at an angle. How much a particular pot will shorten your plant hanger is difficult to predict as it depends on the pot's exact size and shape. In general, the larger and wider the pot, the greater this shortening effect. If, however, the rope you use to make your plant hanger is stretchy, as in the Circle Game Plant Hanger (page 58), then the weight of the pot may stretch the ropes out enough to counteract this effect. If your length requirements are very specific, you may wish to wait to cut the fringe at the bottom until after you have placed your pot inside so that you can tailor the fringe length precisely to your space.

# BEGINNING YOUR PLANT HANGER

In this chapter, you'll find several variations on the plant hanger theme. Each one begins using the method below.

**KNOT**
Square Knot (SK),
page 25

**SUGGESTED SETUP**
Hook or Supported Dowel,
page 18

**SUPPLIES**
Ring listed in pattern

S-hook (optional)

Swivel clip (optional)

Rope listed in pattern,
cut to length

## METHOD

**1** Hang the ring on a secured hook or an S-hook hung from a supported dowel. If you have a swivel clip, fasten it to the ring before hanging.

**2** Thread all the rope through the ring, bringing the ends together so that the center of each rope rests on the ring. Arrange them so that they lie as flatly and neatly as possible. [A]

**3** Find the two outermost cords coming out of the back of the ring. Work 2 SKs, using these two cords as your working cords and all remaining cords as filler. [B]

# SINGLE PLANT HANGER +

Made with 3-ply cotton rope and a shiny brass ring, this plant hanger is a playful variant of the first one I made that spring afternoon in my mom's kitchen. Although I've altered this pattern again and again through the years, I still appreciate the sweet simplicity of my initial try. These days it lives in my upstairs bath, holding aloft a philodendron that doubles as an audience for my shower-singing sessions.

**FINISHED SIZE**
38" long, empty, from top of ring to bottom of fringe

**KNOTS & TECHNIQUES**
Half Square Knot (HSK), page 24

Square Knot (SK), page 25

Sinnet of Square Knots, page 27

Half Square Knot Spiral, page 27

Alternating Square Knots (ASK), page 28

Alternating Rounds of Square Knots, page 29

**SUPPLIES**
99' white 3-ply cotton rope (5mm diameter)

1¼" brass ring

**CUT LIST**
Six 16.5' lengths

CONTINUED

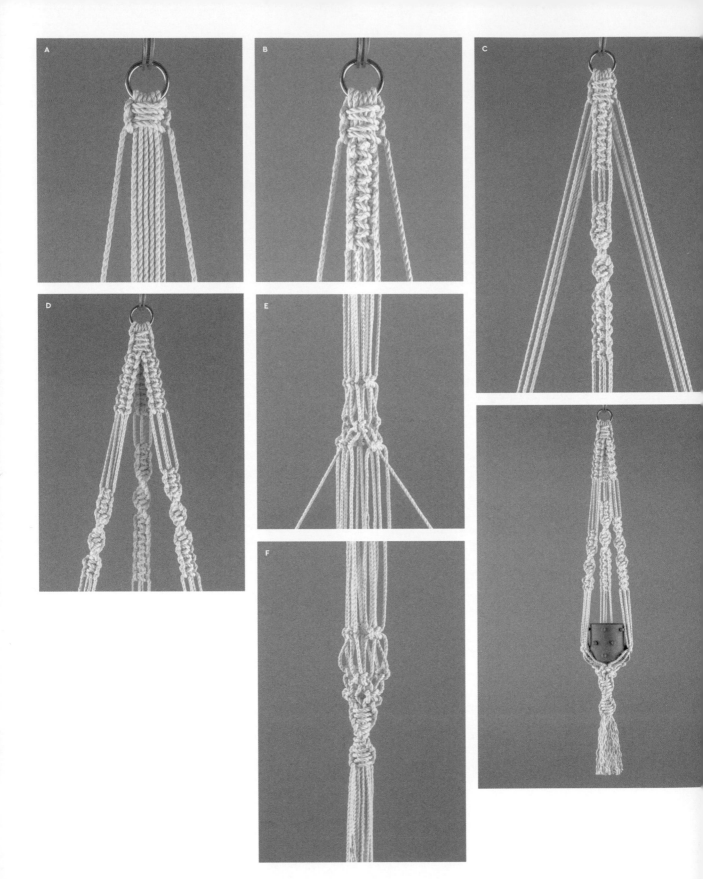

## KNOTTING

1 Complete "Beginning Your Plant Hanger" (page 45). [A]

2 With the SKs facing you, pick up the 4 frontmost cords that are closest to the center. Work a sinnet of 6 SKs using these cords. [B]

3 2" below, work a column consisting of 2 SKs, a spiral of 12 HSKs, and then 6 SKs. [C]

4 Turn your work so that the opposite side is facing you, and divide the remaining 8 cords into two groups of 4, making sure none of them are twisted around each other. Work a sinnet of 6 SKs with each group.

5 4" below the sinnet on your right, work a column consisting of 2 SKs, a spiral of 12 HSKs, and then 4 SKs.

6 Next, 5½" below the sinnet on the left, work a column consisting of 2 SKs, a spiral of 12 HSKs, and then 2 SKs. At this point, the lowest knots you've worked should line up with each other vertically. If they are not even, take a moment to adjust your knotting. [D]

7 6" below, work a round of SKs.

8 To form the basket, work a round of ASKs 2" below the previous round and then a second round of ASKs directly below that. [E]

9 Find the 2 longest remaining cords and use them to work a spiral of 12 HSKs around all other remaining cords. [F]

## FINISHING

10 Trim all cords 6" below the lowest knot.

11 Unravel the cords.

# DOUBLE PLANT HANGER +

If filling your space with plants is a top priority, a double plant hanger will quickly get you on your way. I have one in my kitchen with an easy-to-care-for spider plant cascading down from the top section and a basket of fruit within arm's reach: functional beauty.

**FINISHED SIZE**
68" long, empty, from top of ring to bottom of fringe

**KNOTS & TECHNIQUES**
Square Knot (SK), page 25

Sinnet of Square Knots, page 27

Alternating Square Knots (ASK), page 28

Alternating Rounds of Square Knots, page 29

Alternating Rows/Rounds of Two (or More) Square Knots, page 29

Beading, page 33

**SUPPLIES**
132' white cotton rope (5mm diameter)

1¼" brass ring

Ceramic bead (1½" diameter, 1" hole)

Washi or masking tape

**CUT LIST**
Six 22' lengths

CONTINUED

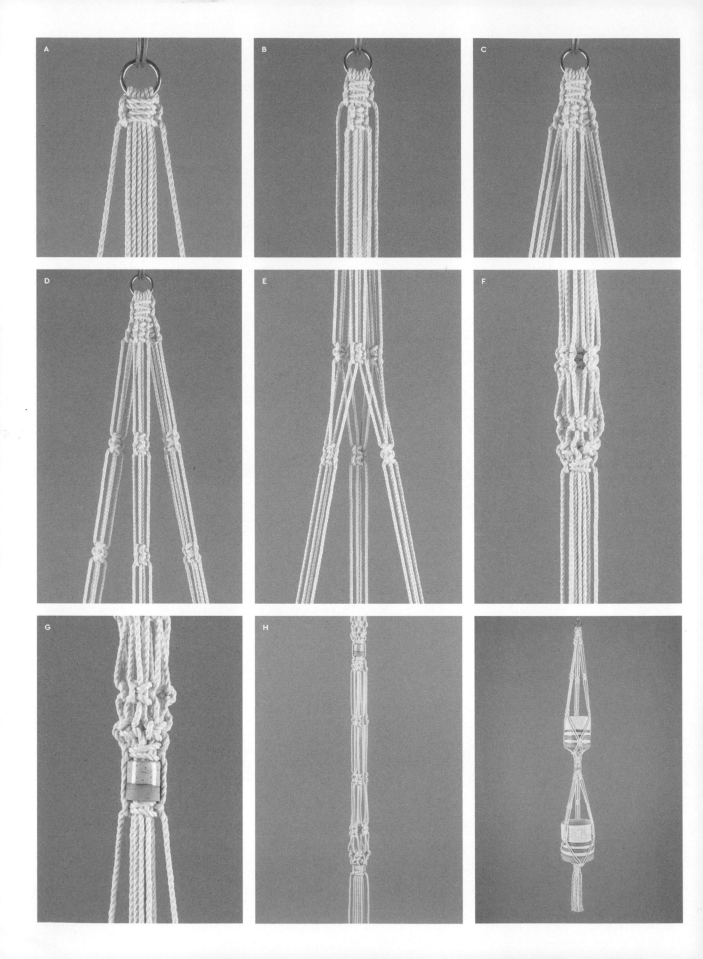

## KNOTTING

**1** Complete "Beginning Your Plant Hanger" (page 45). [A]

**2** With the SKs facing you, pick up the 4 frontmost cords that are closest to the center. Use these cords to work a sinnet of 2 SKs. [B]

**3** Divide the remaining 8 ropes into two groups of 4, making sure none of them are twisted around each other, and work a sinnet of 2 SKs with each group. [C]

**4** 6" below, work a round of 2 SKs. Repeat. [D]

**5** 6" below, begin to form the basket by working an alternating round of 2 SKs. [E]

**6** 2½" below, work a round of ASKs.

**7** 1" below, work a round of ASKs.

**8** Work 1 SK by using 2 of the outermost cords as working cords and the remaining 10 cords as filler. [F]

**9** Tape the ends of the filler cords together. String the bead onto the taped cords, and work an SK below it, using the same working cords as in step 8. [G]

**10** Repeat steps 2–7.

**11** Repeat step 8, this time working 2 SKs. [H]

## FINISHING

**12** Trim all cords 10" below the lowest knot.

**13** Unravel the cords.

# BEADED PLANT HANGER +

When I think of the macramé made popular in the 1970s, jute wall hangings, owls, and plant hangers immediately spring to mind. Here is a modern take on the jute plant hanger, studded with unique handmade beads. The rough texture and warmth of this rope blend naturally into an earthy environment where plants thrive and music fills the air.

**FINISHED SIZE**
58" long, empty, from top of ring to bottom of fringe

**KNOTS & TECHNIQUES**
Square Knot (SK), page 25

Sinnet of Square Knots, page 27

Alternating Square Knots (ASK), page 28

Alternating Rounds of Square Knots, page 29

Alternating Rows/Rounds of Two (or More) Square Knots, page 29

Beading, page 33

**SUPPLIES**
120' jute rope (¼" diameter)

1¼" brass ring

6 wooden beads
(2" long by 1¼" wide, 1" hole)

**CUT LIST**
Six 20' lengths

CONTINUED

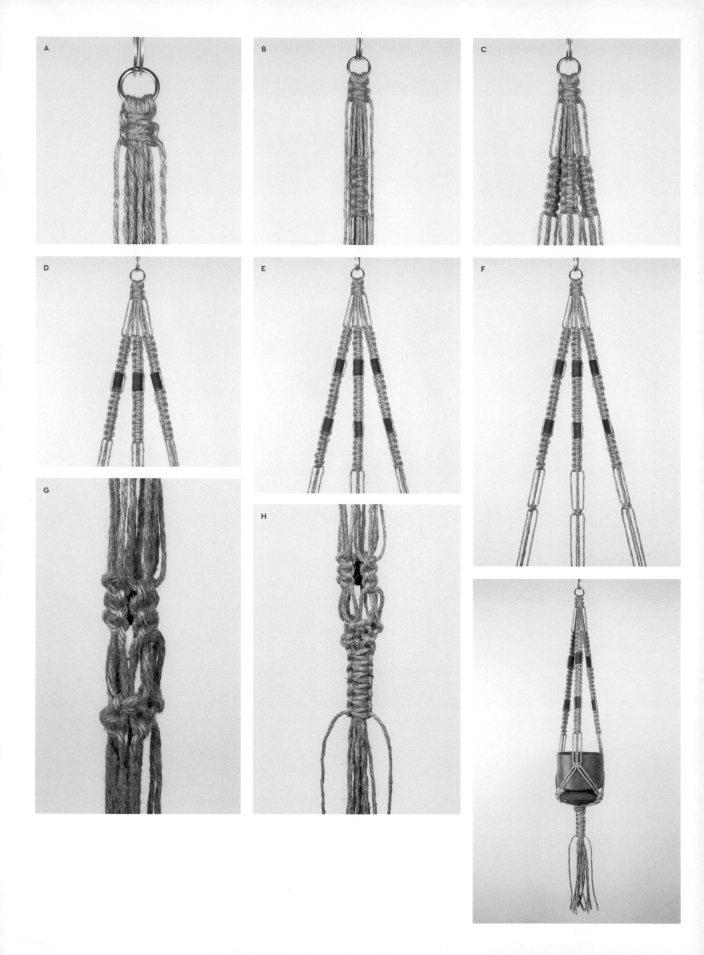

## KNOTTING

1 Complete "Beginning Your Plant Hanger" (page 45). [A]

2 With the SKs facing you, pick up the 4 frontmost cords that are closest to the center. Then, 4" below, use these cords to work a sinnet of 6 SKs. [B]

3 Divide the remaining cords into two groups of 4, and repeat step 2 with each group. [C]

4 Thread a bead onto one set of filler cords, and then work a sinnet of 8 SKs below it. Repeat with the two remaining groups of cords. [D]

5 Thread a second bead onto one of the sets of filler cords, and then work a sinnet of 6 SKs below it. Repeat with the two remaining groups of cords. [E]

6 4" below, work a round of SKs. [F]

7 6" below, begin to form the basket by working an alternating round of 3 SKs.

8 2" below, work a round of ASKs and then a second round of ASKs directly below that. [G]

9 Find two longer cords that are roughly opposite each other. Using these as working cords, work 6 SKs around the remaining cords. [H]

## FINISHING

10 Trim all cords 12" below the lowest knot.

# CIRCLE GAME PLANT HANGER ++

Here, the use of nontraditional materials shifts the mood. Bold and playful, this Scandinavian-inspired plant hanger's round beads and colored stripes will brighten up a dull corner or tie together multiple textures. Hang one among more neutral tones, or make a few in a rainbow of bright shades. It would play well in a child's room, too.

Jersey is stretchy, soft on the hands, and really fun to work with once you get the hang of it; however, it is a bit different to knot than the other materials in this book. Here are a few things to keep in mind.

• When working with a stretchy material, take care to double-check that your knots are lining up properly.

• Watch your cords! The striping of this yarn makes it less obvious when they become twisted.

• When using this yarn, you may occasionally run into a knot made by the manufacturer, joining two ends together. If it won't fit through the center of a bead, simply untie it, slide the bead into place, and retie it securely.

---

**FINISHED SIZE**
80" long, empty, from top of ring to bottom of fringe*

**KNOTS & TECHNIQUES**
Square Knot (SK), page 25

Sinnet of Square Knots, page 27

Alternating Square Knots (ASK), page 28

Alternating Rounds of Square Knots, page 29

Alternating Rows/Rounds of Two (or More) Square Knots, page 29

Beading, page 33

**SUPPLIES**
160' Wool and the Gang "Jersey Be Good" yarn

3" wooden ring

8 spherical wooden beads (⅞" diameter, ⅜" hole)

4 spherical wooden beads (1½" diameter, ½" hole)

**CUT LIST**
Eight 20' lengths

---

*Due to this yarn's stretchiness, the weight of a pot may increase the total length of the plant hanger by several inches.

CONTINUED

## KNOTTING

**1** Complete "Beginning Your Plant Hanger" (page 45). [A]

**2** With the SKs facing you, pick up the 4 frontmost cords that are closest to the center. Use these cords to work a sinnet of 2 SKs.

**3** Divide the remaining 12 ropes into three groups of 4, making sure none of them are twisted around each other, and work a sinnet of 2 SKs with each group.

**4** 4" below, work a round of 3 SKs. [B]

**5** 4" below, work a round of 4 SKs.

**6** Thread a ⅞" bead onto one set of filler cords and work a sinnet of 2 SKs below it. Repeat with the remaining groups of cords.

**7** Thread a 1½" bead onto one set of filler cords, and work a sinnet of 4 SKs below it to secure it in place. Repeat with the remaining groups of cords. [C]

**8** 4" below, work a round of 3 SKs.

**9** 4" below, work a round of 2 SKs. [D]

**10** 4" below, begin to form the basket by working an alternating round of 3 SKs.

**11** 1" below, work a round of ASKs, and then work another row of ASKs directly below that.

**12** Find two longer cords roughly opposite each other and work 3 SKs using these as working cords and all remaining cords as filler. [E]

**13** Select 4 adjacent cords, making sure that the group includes at least 2 of the longest cords. Using these as working cords, work a sinnet of 6 SKs.

**14** Thread a ⅞" bead onto the filler cords and work a sinnet of 8 SKs below it.

**15** Thread another ⅞" bead onto the same cords, and work a sinnet of 3 SKs below it.

**16** Select 4 adjacent cords on the opposite side, again making sure 2 of them are among the longest remaining cords. Using these as working cords, work a sinnet of 10 SKs.

**17** Thread a ⅞" bead onto the filler cords of that sinnet and work a sinnet of 2 SKs below it.

**18** 2" below, work a sinnet of 2 SKs.

**19** Thread another ⅞" bead onto the same filler cords and work 4 SKs below it.

## FINISHING

**20** Trim the fringe into a ponytail shape.

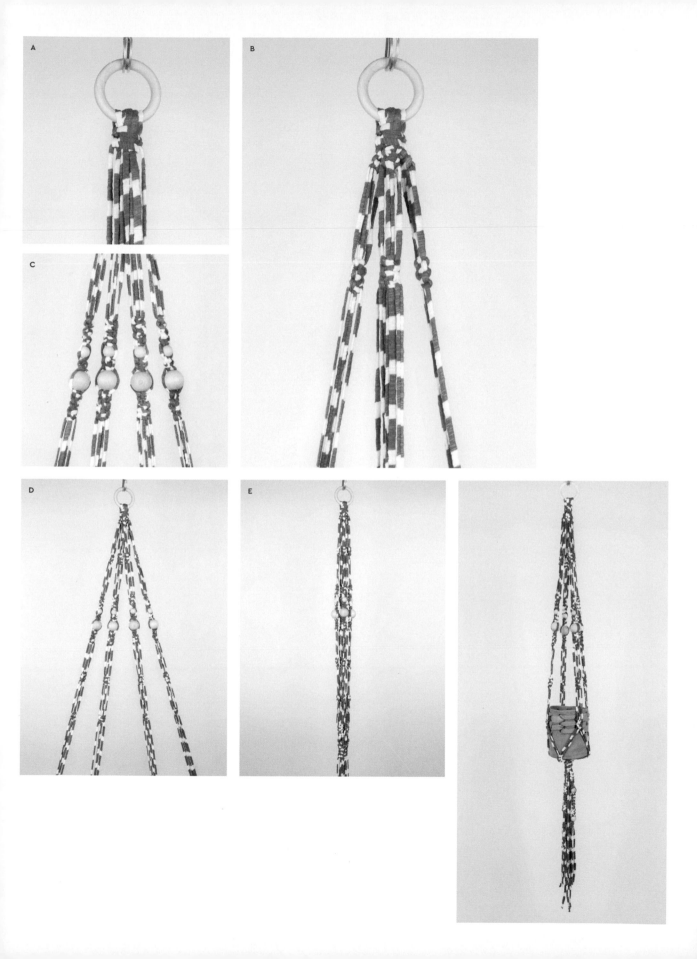

# NATURE CHANNEL PLANT HANGER ++

Sometimes the design for a piece is built around the vessel that will hang in it. Sometimes the material is what dictates the design. This army green/gray twine called out to be a simple and pretty hanger, and why resist? A light-colored pot works especially well here, showing off the woodsy-toned knotwork.

**FINISHED SIZE**
39" long, empty, from top of ring to bottom of fringe

**KNOTS & TECHNIQUES**
Square Knot (SK), page 25

Sinnet of Square Knots, page 27

Alternating Square Knots (ASK), page 28

Alternating Rounds of Square Knots, page 29

Alternating Rows/Rounds of Two (or More) Square Knots, page 29

**SUPPLIES**
96' hemp gardening cord (⅛" diameter)

1¼" brass ring

3" brass ring

**CUT LIST**
Eight 12' lengths

CONTINUED

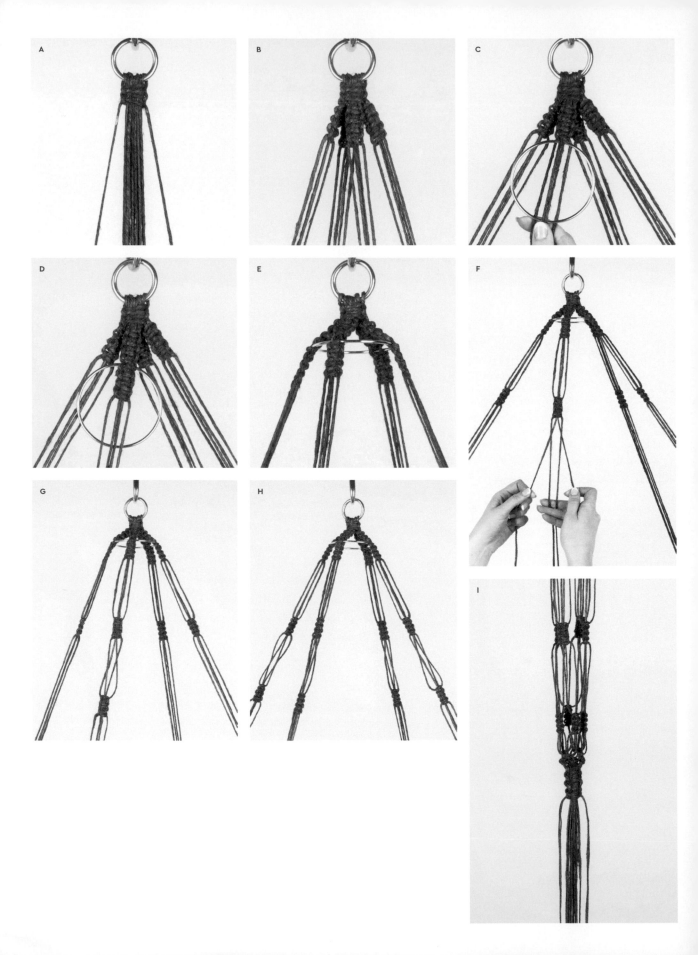

## KNOTTING

**1** Complete "Beginning Your Plant Hanger" (page 45) using the 1¼" brass ring. [A]

**2** With the SKs facing you, pick up the 4 frontmost cords that are closest to the center. Use these cords to work a sinnet of 4 SKs.

**3** Divide the remaining 12 cords into three groups of 4, making sure none of them are twisted around each other, and work a sinnet of 4 SKs with each group. [B]

**4** Hold the 3" ring so that its edge rests just below an SK from the previous round. Mount the cords onto the ring by bringing the filler cords to the front [C] and then working a sinnet of 4 SKs [D].

**5** Repeat step 4 on the opposite side so that the ring hangs horizontally.

**6** Repeat with the remaining two groups of 4 cords. [E]

**7** 4" below each sinnet, work another sinnet of 4 SKs.

**8** Swap the working and filler cords [F] and work another sinnet of 4 SKs 4" below the previous one [G]. Repeat with the remaining cords. [H]

**9** Repeat step 7.

**10** 4" below, begin to form the basket by working an alternating round of 4 SKs.

**11** Next, 1½" below, work a round of ASKs.

**12** Work another round of ASKs directly below the previous one.

**13** Find two pairs of longer cords that are hanging roughly opposite each other, and use them, held double, to work 4 SKs around the remaining cords. [I]

## FINISHING

**14** Trim all cords 6" below the lowest knot.

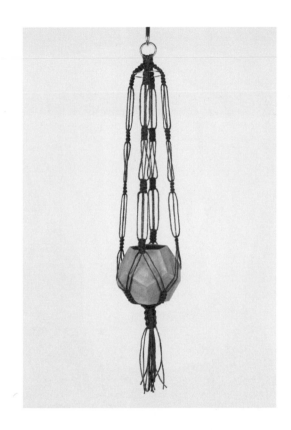

# HANGING BASKET ++

I originally envisioned this delicate basket holding a jar of spoons in the kitchen; but since then, it has proven more versatile than I thought, working stints as a produce bag, a hanging vase, and even a paintbrush holder.

It makes a pretty plant hanger, too. As is, it will house a small, delicate specimen; enlarged and made with rope, it could hold a more substantial pot or vase. If you'd like to change the basket's size or material, see How Long Should the Ropes Be? (page 34) for help calculating your rope lengths.

**FINISHED SIZE**
17" long by 6" wide, laid flat

**KNOTS & TECHNIQUES**
Reverse Lark's Head Knot (RLHK), page 23

Square Knot (SK), page 25

Sinnet of Square Knots, page 27

Alternating Square Knots (ASK), page 28

Alternating Rounds of Square Knots, page 29

**SUGGESTED SETUPS**
Note: This project starts from one type of setup and then moves to another.

Corkboard and Pins, page 18

Hanging Dowel or Hook, page 18

**SUPPLIES**
240' fine hemp twine

Vase or quart-size mason jar with circular bottom (approximately 7" tall by 3½" diameter)

Paper and pencil

Scissors

Swivel clip

S-hook

Darning needle

**CUT LIST**
Sixteen 15' lengths

CONTINUED

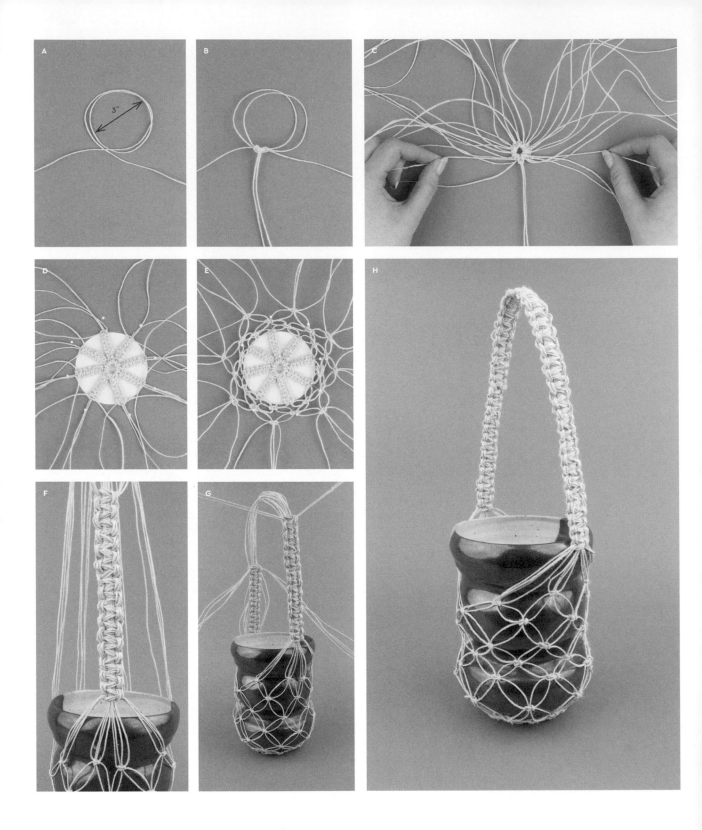

## BASE

1 Fold one 15' length in half and make a small, doubled-over loop at its center. You will want the diameter of this loop to be about 3". [A]

2 Use an RLHK to mount a 15' rope onto the loop where the cords cross. Keep track of the 2 cords of the loop. [B]

3 Mount all of the remaining ropes onto the loop using RLHKs. It is fine if the loop stretches out a bit as you do this.

4 Find the 2 cords you used to make the original loop. Take a moment to make sure they are the same length, and adjust if necessary. Grasp one in each hand and pull in opposite directions to close the loop. [C]

5 Trace the bottom of the vase onto a piece of paper. Cut out the shape, set it on the corkboard, and pin the loop at its center.

6 Again, find the 2 cords you used to form the loop. Using these as working cords and the 2 cords between them as filler cords, work a sinnet of SKs that reaches the edge of the paper. Repeat with the remaining cords.

7 Space the sinnets evenly around the paper's edge and pin in place. [D]

## BODY

8 Work 3 rounds of ASKs, leaving enough room between the knots to allow the knotting to lie flat. Once you are satisfied with a knot's placement, give the working cords an extra tug to firmly secure the knot in place before moving on. (Alternating knots in this material may require a little extra tightening to stay in place.) [E]

9 Remove all the pins, attach the swivel clip to the center of your work, and hang it from a secured dowel or hook.

10 Continue working ASKs until the knots reach your desired height. After every couple of rounds, place the vase in the basket to make sure it fits properly. The basket should roughly conform to the shape of the vase without being overly snug.

11 Remove the swivel clip and place the vase inside the basket.

## STRAP

12 Divide the cords in half. Starting about 1" above the rim of the vase, work a sinnet of 15 SKs holding 4 cords at a time. [F]

13 Repeat step 12 on the opposite side, using the remaining 16 cords.

14 Overlap the two sets of filler cords by about 6", making an arch. [G]

15 Use the upper set of working cords to work SKs around both sets of filler cords until the strap is covered.

## FINISHING

16 Cut the ends of all cords to 6" and tuck them into the knotting with the darning needle. [H]

# PLANT OR FLORAL DISPLAY ++

When I moved into my studio, the first thing I did was hang a piece of driftwood from the ceiling to work from and serve as a visual focal point. When I finished a piece and the branch hung empty, I would style a photo to document my handmade goods, hanging them from that special piece of wood.

One day, it held five different styles of plant hangers, populated with an array of ceramics, a selection of favorite plants, and, in one vase, a few wide-eyed Stargazer lily stems. The simple iPhone image I snapped of this colorful group took off on Pinterest like none I'd taken before! It just goes to show that sometimes the whole truly is more than the sum of its parts.

But how do you pick the right parts and how is it best to arrange them? This is just one road map to making some special plant hangers even more special together. I've also placed them over a dining table as pictured on page 73, but your crowd of beauties might light up any number of spaces in your home.

**SUPPLIES**

Your favorite branch, dowel, or rod (about 5' long by 2" diameter)

2–4 screw eyes; 2 for the ceiling, 2 for the branch (optional)

Rope, aircraft cable, or sturdy cordage

S-hooks

Selection of pots or vases

Plant hangers, various sizes

Plants (and cut flowers or foliage, if desired)

CONTINUED

## SELECTING A BRANCH

• Select a branch that is strong and has a nice shape. I prefer ones that are mostly straight, but choose what speaks to you.

• Explore your environment! Foraging near a river or favorite beach is an excellent way to spend an afternoon, and fallen branches from a nearby forest work wonderfully as well.

• If your style is more modern, try a clean birch dowel from the hardware store, a metal support beam, or a copper or acrylic rod.

## CHOOSING THE VESSELS

Choose plant pots or vases that:

• Don't have drainage holes, or do have built-in saucers. That way you'll avoid spillage when watering.

• Vibe with your interior. From simple terra-cotta planters to handmade options with interesting glazes, a variety of styles and shapes will add visual interest.

• Fit the plant hanger. Most of the plant-hanger patterns in this book will fit a range of pot sizes, from 4 inches all the way to 12 inches in diameter. If you have a much larger planter, simply adjust the row spacing at the base of your plant hanger to fit.

## PAIRING WITH PLANTS

The shapes of the plants or flowers are just as important as the spacing of the hangers. From big leafy philodendrons to more twig-like cacti, or from the wandering Jew's leggy purple vines to an architectural jade, macramé really was made to pair with plants. I like to arrange flora so that they stretch out of their knotted hangers reaching toward the light.

When selecting potted plants for your display, don't forget to consider whether the space you've chosen can give them what they need to thrive, be it bright or filtered sunlight, shade, humidity, or drier air. This will set you up to succeed and might help you to narrow your houseplant options.

Floral arrangements also do really well in this configuration. Imagine a wedding table with flowers dripping overhead, a dinner party beneath a cascade of tropical bouquets, or a birthday celebration with locally foraged branches suspended from a big tree above, dappling shade and whimsy over a patterned picnic blanket.

## INSTALLATION

Once you've gathered everything you need, you are ready to install your display. Make sure your hardware is intended to hold the combined weight of your branch, plant hangers, and (heaviest of all) potted plants. Remember also that potted plants are at their heaviest just after being watered. Always ask for help at your local hardware store if you have any questions. Then follow the steps below.

• Install two screw eyes into the ceiling, making sure they are each screwed securely into a stud. If desired, screw the remaining screw eyes into the branch parallel to each other.

• Use rope, aircraft cable, or other sturdy cordage to hang the wood from the eye hooks at your desired height.

## ARRANGING YOUR HANGINGS

I like to style these arrangements with an odd number of plant hangers and a mix of macramé styles and sizes. Use an S-hook to hang each one from the branch. This makes height adjustments quick and easy. Space out the hangers across the branch, and try a few different configurations until you land on one that feels right.

Once you have your branch and plant hangers ready to go, it is time to set the pots or vases into the macramé. You will want to have your plants potted and bouquets arranged before doing this (although with florals, you can add more dramatic stems after the pieces are hung). A thoughtfully placed lily, or the giant leaf of a monstera tucked into a vase, is a stunning choice, and might be that last detail that pulls it all together.

# WALL HANGINGS AND MORE

Some walls wish to be left empty. Others beg for embellishment. This chapter has seven projects to reinvent a variety of spaces. From the simple and elegant Gold Dust Woman Wall Hanging, with its textural interest and shiny brass accents, to the I Am Not Dreaming Tent, a more conceptual "wall hanging," you will find something for nearly every room in the house. Utilizing a variety of knots, these projects show the breadth of what macramé can do to adorn your life with the handmade.

The Celebration Garland (page 80), draped above a daybed covered by a voluptuous sheepskin and patterned throw pillows, is the definition of hygge in this light-filled reading nook.

Hanging from the beams of a painted-white A-frame, the Summer Solstice Mobile (page 88) is a beautiful object to wake up to. While, tucked in the corner, the Basket (page 235) holds extra blankets.

# CELEBRATION GARLAND +

I often dream of dining under macramé garlands—the knotwork dressing up the party. In the fall of 2016, my dear friend Alexis Davis and I hosted our first Macramé and Meditation Retreat in the desert near Joshua Tree, and one of the projects all the participants made together was a garland like this one. We worked collaboratively, each adding bits of color and letting the design come together as it would. The feeling was so warm, communal, magical, and, naturally, festive!

In terms of construction, this garland is essentially a string of tiny wall hangings. The pattern includes two different mini-panel designs. You can either arrange them in the order given or mix and match as you see fit. A few simple variations are listed as well, or feel free to come up with your own! And of course, this is a perfect project to work on with friends, even those who've never done macramé before.

**FINISHED SIZE**
13–16' wide stretched taut, depending on panel placement, by 26" long at longest point, including fringe

**KNOTS & TECHNIQUES**
Reverse Lark's Head Knot (RLHK), page 23

Square Knot (SK), page 25

Right-Facing Square Knot (RSK), page 25

Sinnet of Square Knots, page 27

Sinnet of Right-Facing Square Knots, page 27

Alternating Square Knots (ASK), page 28

Alternating Rows of Square Knots, page 29

**SUGGESTED SETUP**
Supported Dowel or Hanging Dowel, page 18

**SUPPLIES**
Main Color Rope (MC): 720' white cotton rope (5mm diameter)

Contrast Color Rope (CC): 40' dyed cotton rope (5mm diameter)

**CUT LIST**
Two 20' lengths in MC

Sixty-eight 10' lengths in MC

Four 10' lengths in CC

CONTINUED

## PREPARATION

1 Hold the two 20' MC ropes together. These serve as the mounting cords for the garland. Leaving a tail of several feet, securely tie them onto the dowel. Use any knot you'd like here, as it will be removed later.

2 Tie the ropes to the dowel a second time, leaving about 2' of rope between the two attachment points.

## LARGE PANELS

3 Using RLHKs, mount 10' ropes onto the mounting cords (*not* the dowel) in the following order, from left to right: 5 in MC, 2 in CC, 5 in MC. Space them evenly across a 16" length of mounting cord.

Work the following rows 1¼" apart.

Row 1: Skip 2 cords, work 5 SKs, then skip 2 cords.

Row 2: Work 2 SKs, 1 RSK, then 3 SKs.

Row 3: Repeat Row 1.

Row 4: Repeat Row 2.

Row 5: Skip 2 cords, work 5 sinnets of 2 SKs, then skip 2 cords.

Row 6: Skip 4 cords, work 1 SK, 1 RSK, 2 SKs, then skip 4 cords.

Row 7: Skip 6 cords, work 3 SKs, then skip 6 cords.

Row 8: Skip 8 cords, work 1 RSK, 1 SK, then skip 8 cords.

Row 9: Use the CC cords to work a sinnet of 3 SKs.

Trim all cords about 10" below their last respective knot and unravel them.

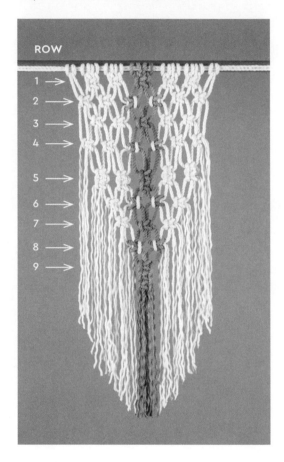

4 Retie the mounting cords to the dowel to make a new 2' working area to one side of the panel you just worked.

5 Repeat step 3 to work a second Large Panel.

## SMALL PANELS

**6** Retie the mounting cords to the dowel to make a new 2' working area to one side of the two large panels.

**7** Mount 8 MC ropes using RLHKs. Space them evenly across a 10" length of the mounting cord.

Work the following rows 1" apart.

Rows 1–3: Work 3 rows of ASKs.

Row 4: Skip 2 cords, work 3 SKs, then skip 2 cords.

Row 5: Skip 4 cords, work 2 sinnets of 2 SKs, then skip 4 cords.

Row 6: Skip 6 cords, work a sinnet of 2 SKs, then skip 6 cords.

Trim all cords 8" below their last respective knots, and unravel them. You will have a lot of extra rope at this point. Set this aside for use in step 10.

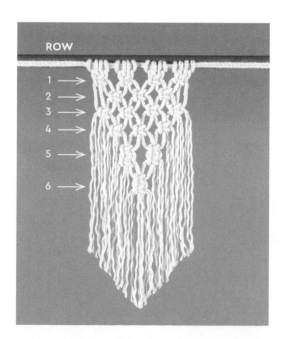

**8** Repeat steps 6–7 until you have three small panels on either side of the two large panels.

## FINISHING

**9** Space the panels out along the mounting cords, leaving as much or as little room between them as you'd like. Just be sure to leave enough excess mounting cord at either end to tie your finished garland in place when you install it.

**10** Using RLHKs, mount the ropes you have set aside between the panels as desired. Add as many as you'd like, trim to suit, and unravel them.

## VARIATIONS

MAKE SHORTER, TRIANGULAR PANELS: Skip the first three rows of knotting on each large panel and the first two rows of each small panel.

SHORTER PANELS WITH A DENSER LOOK: Group the working cords closer together on the mounting cord and leave less space between rows.

MIX AND MATCH THE PANELS: Be sure to adjust the length of the mounting cords if you'd like to change the overall length of your garland.

TRY STRIPING AND DIFFERENT COLOR COMBINATIONS: You could use multiple colors and/or materials, or skip the striping altogether.

# GOLD DUST WOMAN WALL HANGING ++

In this piece, the combination of thick cotton rope and hand-felted wool yarn brings depth and interest, while oversize brass beads deliver a tasteful hint of glamour.

The wool yarn (CC) used in this pattern has some give to it. As a result, knots made from it will vary in size depending upon the degree to which you tighten them, with knots tightened firmly being significantly smaller than those made with a more relaxed tension. In this project, some knots worked in this material should be smaller than others. This will be specified in the row-by-row instructions. All knots worked in the cotton rope (MC), on the other hand, should be tightened firmly.

**FINISHED SIZE**
24–28" wide by 36" long, including fringe

**KNOTS & TECHNIQUES**
Reverse Lark's Head Knot (RLHK), page 23

Square Knot (SK), page 25

Right-Facing Square Knot (RSK), page 25

Mounting with a Square Knot, see page 26

Sinnet of Square Knots, page 27

Sinnet of Right-Facing Square Knots, page 27

Alternating Rows of Square Knots, page 29

Overhand Knot (OK), page 33

**SUGGESTED SETUP**
Supported Dowel or Hanging Dowel, page 18

**SUPPLIES**
Main Color Rope (MC): 100' twisted 3-ply cotton rope (½" diameter)

Contrast Color Rope (CC): 100' Love Fest Fibers "Tough Love" felt yarn in Natural

6' round leather cord (1mm diameter)

Washi or masking tape

24–28" driftwood branch

Two S-hooks

Six 2"-square brass beads

**CUT LIST**
Four 14' lengths in MC

Four 10' lengths in MC

One 4' length in MC

Four 25' lengths in CC

Six 1' lengths leather cord

CONTINUED

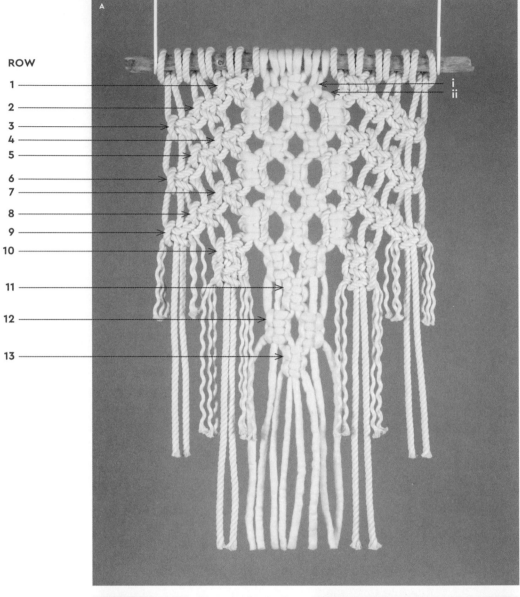

1     i
2     ii
3
4
5
6
7
8
9
10
11
12
13

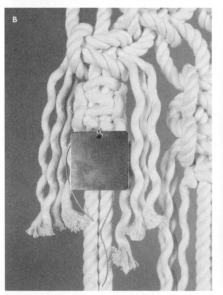

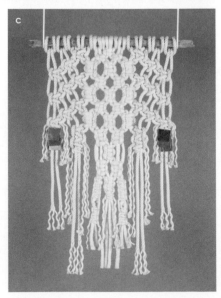

## PREPARATION

1 Wrap the ends of the MC rope with tape to keep them from unraveling.

2 Hang the driftwood branch from the dowel using the S-hooks spaced 22" apart.

3 Using RLHKs, mount the ropes onto the branch between the S-hooks in the following order: two 10' MC, two 14' MC, four 25' CC, two 14' MC, and then two 10' MC.

## KNOTTING

4 Work the following rows from left to right.

Row 1: Skip 4 cords, work an SK, skip the 8 CC cords, work an RSK, and skip the last 4 cords. Then knot the 8 CC cords at the center as follows.

 i. Work an SK in the center, tightening it firmly so that its height is about half that of the SKs you worked in MC.

 ii. Work an SK and then an RSK in a row directly below, tightening them firmly. Make sure the bottoms of these two knots line up with the bottoms of those you worked in MC. Adjust as needed.

Row 2: Skip 2 cords, work an SK, work an RSK, work 2 SKs in a row, work an RSK, skip the last 2 cords. These knots should line up horizontally regardless of material.

Row 3: Work an SK, skip 2 cords, work an RSK, work 2 SKs in a row, skip 2 cords, work an RSK. These knots should line up horizontally as well.

Row 4: Skip 4 cords, work an SK. Then in CC, work a sinnet of 2 SKs and then a sinnet of 2 RSKs, both tightened firmly. Then work an RSK, skip the last 4 cords.

Rows 5–7: Repeat Rows 2–4.

Rows 8–9: Repeat Rows 2–3.

Row 10: Skip 4 cords, work 2 sinnets of 2 SKs, work 2 sinnets of 2 RSKs, and then skip 4 cords. From this row on, work knots in CC using a moderate tension. They do not need to line up precisely with those made in MC.

Row 11: Work a sinnet of 2 SKs using the centermost 4 cords.

Row 12: Skip 8 cords, work a sinnet of 2 SKs, work a sinnet of 2 RSKs, and then skip 8 cords.

Row 13: Repeat Row 11.

5 Trim the leftmost 8 cords to the following lengths, from left to right: 5", 16", 16", 5", 10", 20", 20", 10". Trim the rightmost 8 cords to mirror those on the left. Cut straight across the CC cords in the center, in line with the longest MC cords. Unravel the plies of the MC working cords. Do not discard the trimmings. [A]

6 Untwist the 4' MC rope into three separate plies. Do the same with the 2 longest scraps you trimmed in step 5. For the remaining knotting, you will use these plies individually, and as you choose.

7 Mount the separated plies one at a time onto the pairs of filler cords using SKs; then work additional SKs as desired. Be creative! Your knotting does not have to be exactly like mine. Just make sure to work an additional 2 SKs (or more) on the left- and rightmost columns, onto which to mount your beading.

8 Use RLHKs to mount a 1' length of leather cord onto each bead.

9 Tie each bead onto one of the single-ply SKs on the far left and right using 2 OKs. [B]

## FINISHING

10 Trim and unravel the cords as desired. [C]

# SUMMER SOLSTICE MOBILE ++

When I was in fifth grade, my class took a rafting trip on the John Day River in eastern Oregon. We camped for three nights, singing around the fire and watching the moonrise. During the day, we floated down the river, learned crafts, and foraged in the surrounding forest for huckleberries, wildflowers, and art materials. Later, we stared into the mystery of the sky, naming constellations and whispering with friends into the wee hours. This mobile is inspired by artist Alexander Calder, outer space, and memories from that rafting trip in Oregon.

**FINISHED SIZE**
18" diameter, plus up to 18" fringe

**KNOTS & TECHNIQUES**
Reverse Lark's Head Knot (RLHK), page 23

Square Knot (SK), page 25

Mounting with a Square Knot (SK), see page 26

Sinnet of Square Knots, page 27

Overhand Knot (OK), page 33

**SUGGESTED SETUP**
Supported Dowel or Hook, page 18

**SUPPLIES**
128' white cotton rope (5mm diameter)

40" fine hemp twine

18" metal hoop

12" metal hoop

12 brass bugle beads

S-hook

Swivel clip

**CUT LIST**
Four 12' lengths white cotton rope for ropes D, E, F, H*

Eight 10' lengths white cotton rope for ropes A, B, C, G, I, J, K, L*

Two 20" lengths fine hemp twine

*See diagram on page 93.

CONTINUED

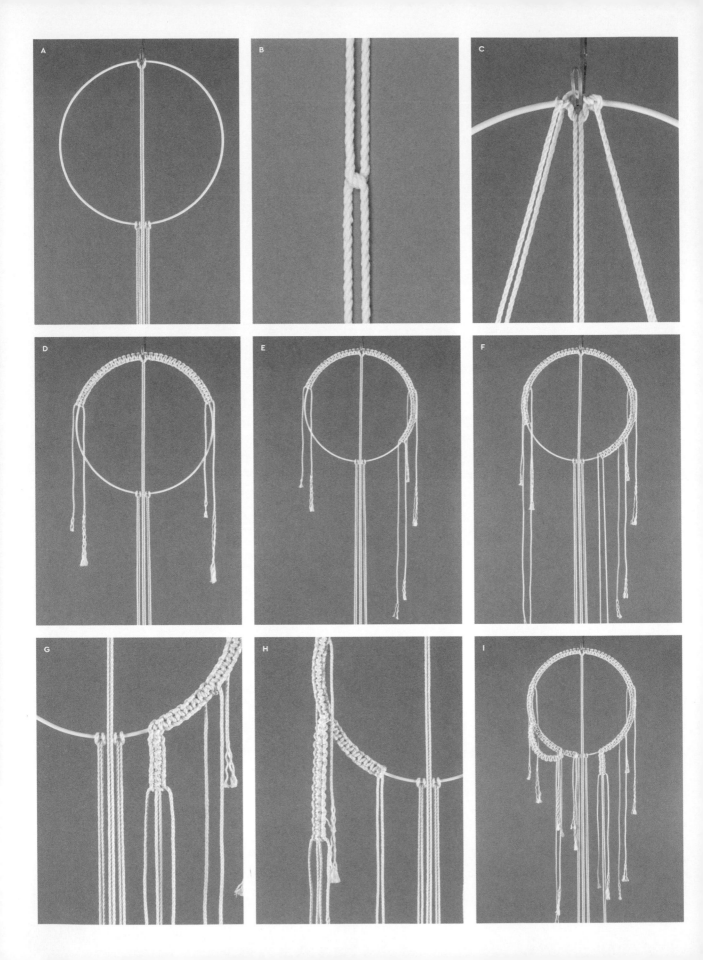

## PREPARATION

1 Fold each rope in half and organize by length.

2 Hang the S-hook from the dowel or hook, and hang the 18" hoop from the S-hook.

## KNOTTING

Before mounting each rope, check its length in the Cut List and its positioning in the diagram on page 93.

3 Mount ropes A, B, and C onto the hoop using RLHKs. Hang your work by looping the S-hook through the RLHK at the top of A. [A]

4 Link ropes D and E together at the center. [B]

5 Mount D and E onto the hoop on either side of A using SKs, centering the link between them over A. [C]

6 Work SKs counterclockwise around the hoop with rope D until about 9" of rope remain on each of its cords. It is okay if the cords are not exactly the same length.

7 Repeat step 6 on the right with rope E. [D]

8 Using an SK, mount F onto the hoop where indicated on the chart and work around clockwise until you have made about 14 SKs in all, or until about 7" of bare hoop remain between the last knot worked and C. [E]

9 Mount H onto the hoop with an SK and work another 11 SKs counterclockwise around the hoop.

10 Mount rope G with an SK and work another 6 SKs clockwise around the hoop. [F]

11 Fold I in half over the hoop and bring its cords between those of G. Using G's cords as working cords and I's cords as filler cords, work a sinnet of 6 SKs. [G]

12 Fold J in half over the hoop, and bring its cords around those of rope H. Using J's cords as working cords and H's cords as filler cords, work a sinnet of 15 SKs.

13 Mount L with an SK, and use it to work 9 SKs counterclockwise around the hoop. [H]

14 Mount the filler cords from the leftmost sinnet (H and J) onto the hoop using an SK, and work SKs until you reach B, just 2 or 3 more. [I]

CONTINUED

**15**  Use B and C to work a sinnet of 12 SKs. [J]

**16**  Mount K next to C using an SK and use it to cover the remaining segment of exposed hoop with SKs.

**17**  You've come full circle! Mount A onto the 12" hoop with an SK so that it hangs about 2" below the large hoop. If your hoop has a visible seam, use this knot to conceal it. Work 14 SKs clockwise around the small hoop. [K]

## FINISHING

**18**  String the beads onto the lengths of fine hemp twine, securing a few onto either end using OKs.

**19**  Mount one strand of beads onto the smaller hoop using an RLHK.

**20**  Use an RLHK to mount the second strand of beads between F and G.

**21**  Finish the fringe as desired, working a few more SKs and OKs wherever you choose before unraveling the ends. [L]

**22**  Install using a swivel clip attached to an S-hook, so your mobile can rotate freely.

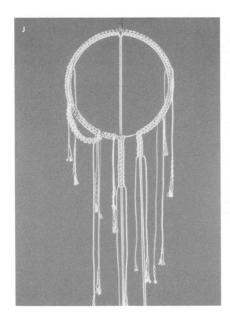
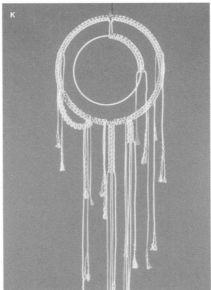

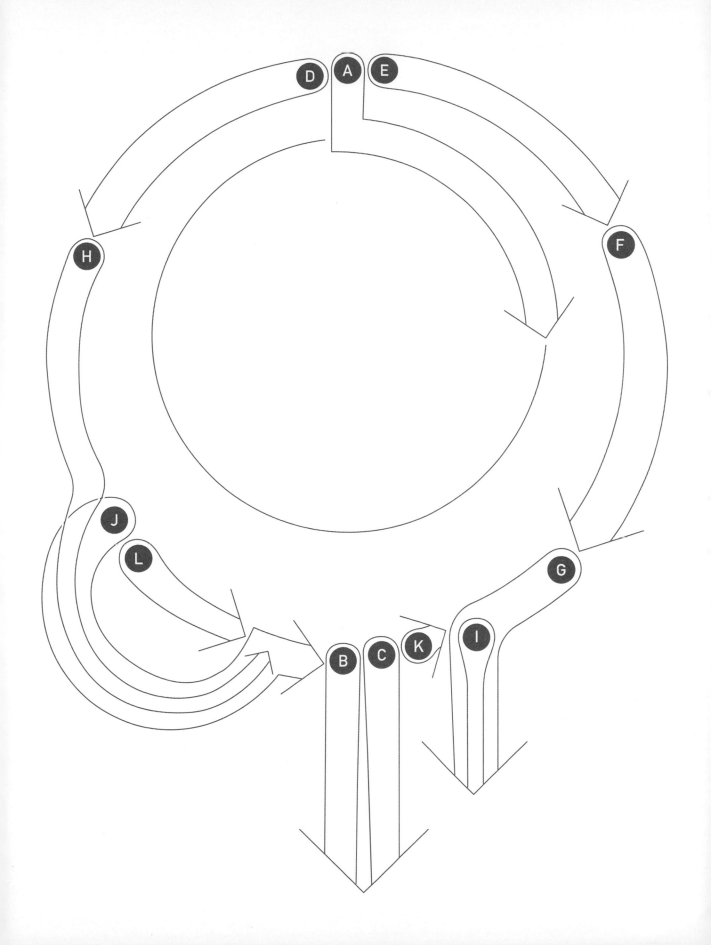

# GEOLOGICAL SHIFT WALL HANGING ++

We live between layers, below the atmosphere and above the strata of the earth. We sleep between layers, too, with the soft clouds of blankets above us and the progressively sturdy tiers of mattress and frame below. This thought inspired an over-the-bed wall hanging, with bands of knotwork varying in color, knot type, material, and density. This piece also makes a solid statement above a sofa, another place to layer yourself between some blankets for some well-earned rest and relaxation.

**FINISHED SIZE**
5' wide by 3'10" long, including fringe

**KNOTS & TECHNIQUES**
Reverse Lark's Head Knot (RLHK), page 23

Square Knot (SK), page 25

Sinnet of Square Knots, page 27

Alternating Square Knots (ASK), page 28

Alternating Rows of Square Knots, page 29

Alternating Rows/Rounds of Two (or More) Square Knots, page 29

Horizontal Double Half Hitch (HDHH), page 30

Vertical Double Half Hitch (VDHH), page 32

Overhand Knot (OK), page 33

**SUGGESTED SETUP**
Supported Dowel or Hanging Dowel, page 18

**SUPPLIES**
Main Color Rope (MC): 780' braided cotton rope in white (½" diameter)

Contrast Color Rope (CC): 584' cotton rope in light gray (5mm diameter)

5' wooden dowel (1¼" diameter)

2 S-hooks

Washi or masking tape

**CUT LIST**
Twenty-six 30' lengths MC

Twelve 36' lengths CC

Four 20' lengths CC

Twelve 6' lengths CC

CONTINUED

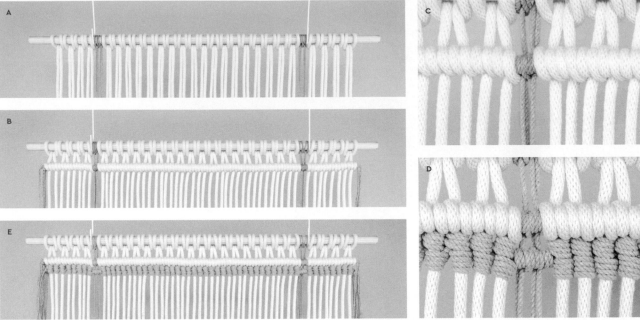

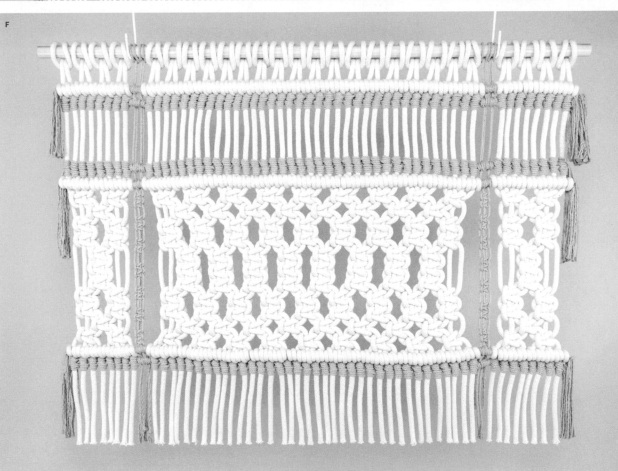

## PREPARATION

1 Hang the S-hooks a few feet apart on the supported dowel, and place the 5' wooden dowel on the hooks.

2 Divide the twelve 6' CC ropes into three groups of 4, and tape each set together at the ends. Repeat with the 36' CC ropes.

## KNOTTING

3 Mount all of the 30' MC ropes onto the dowel using RLHKs.

4 Between the fourth and fifth MC ropes from the left, mount two 20' CC ropes using RLHKs. Repeat on the right. Space all ropes evenly, leaving 3" of space at either end of the dowel. [A]

5 Pick up one set of 6' CC ropes and, leaving a tail of about 8", work a row of HDHHs from left to right around it 2½" below the RLHKs. [B] When you come to the CC cords, use them held double. [C] (If you don't work your HDHHs tightly enough, this row may become wider than desired. Be sure to tighten your HDHHs securely, and make sure that each HDHH you work is directly below the RLHK above it.)

6 Pick up one set of four 36' CC cords. Leaving an 8" tail, use these 4 cords held together to work VDHHs from left to right around the leftmost 8 MC cords. You should now have reached the first group of CC cords. Use these vertically hanging CC cords held double to work HDHHs around the set of 4 CC cords you've used as the working cord up to this point. [D] Complete the rest of the row in the same way, using the set of 4 CC cords to work a VDHH around each MC cord, and using the vertically hanging CC cords held double to work HDHHs. This row looks particularly nice if you take a moment to flatten and organize your cords as you tighten each knot. [E]

7 Then, 6" below, repeat step 6.

8 Directly below, work a row of HDHH around a set of 6' CC cords, as in step 5.

9 Work the following rows using the centermost 36 cords.

Rows 1–2: Work 2 rows of ASKs.

Row 3: Work an alternating row of 2 SKs.

Row 4: Work an alternating row of 3 SKs.

Row 5: Work an alternating row of 2 SKs.

Rows 6–7: Work 2 rows of ASKs.

10 Repeat step 9 using the leftmost 8 cords and then once again on the right.

11 With each of the two groups of 4 CC cords hanging vertically, work a column consisting of 7 sinnets of 2 SKs spaced 1¼" apart. The bottom of these columns should align vertically with the bottom of the MC knotting to this point. If it does not, take a moment to adjust accordingly.

12 Repeat step 5 using the remaining set of four 6' CC cords.

13 Repeat step 6 using the remaining set of four 36' CC cords.

## FINISHING

14 At each end of the rows of HDHHs, tie an OK in one of the CC cords. Tighten the knot securely against the HDHHs, pressing them together.

15 Trim all fringe to 8" and unravel the CC cords. [F]

# RISING SUN DOOR CURTAIN +++

In 2014, Haiti Design Group invited me to Port au Prince to teach their skilled artisans. These weavers, jewelry makers, and leather workers were already adept at many crafts but wanted to add macramé to their repertoire. We spent the week together, eating, laughing, and knotting.

I worked side by side with a craftswoman on a simple door curtain with a stripe of indigo down the center. The result of our collaboration now hangs in my home. As I walk through it daily, I am reminded that kindness and generosity are the best gifts we can hope for in the world.

On my last day, one of the women brought a book to show me, full of macramé patterns written in Creole. She said it was one of her most cherished books. Turning through the pages, I was struck anew by the way in which crafts have their own language, with the power to transcend borders of all kinds. This project is an homage to my experience there.

**FINISHED SIZE**
34" wide by 80" long, including fringe

**KNOTS & TECHNIQUES**
Reverse Lark's Head Knot (RLHK), page 23

Square Knot (SK), page 25

Sinnet of Square Knots page 27

Alternating Rows of Square Knots, page 29

Alternating Rows/Rounds of Two (or More) Square Knots, page 29

Overhand Knot (OK), page 33

**SUGGESTED SETUP**
Hanging Dowel, page 18

**SUPPLIES**
1,096' white cotton rope (5mm diameter)

40"-long dowel, driftwood branch, or curtain rod (1–3" diameter)

Washi or masking tape

**CUT LIST**
Thirty-six 24' lengths

Sixteen 14'6" lengths

CONTINUED

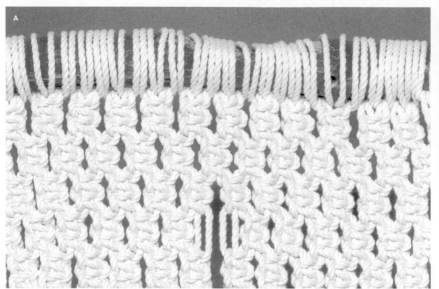

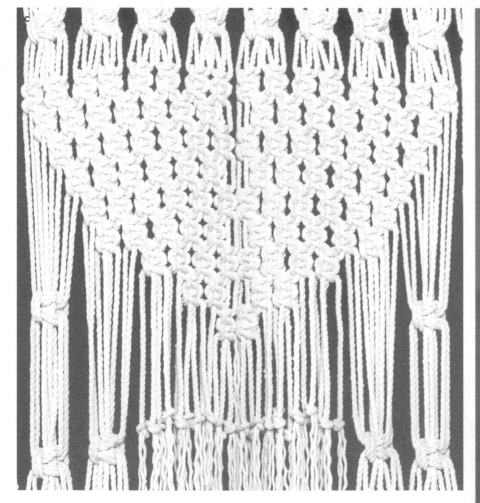

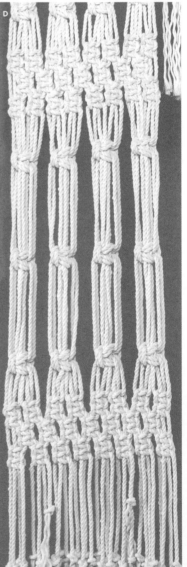

## PREPARATION

1  Tape off a 34" workspace in the center of your dowel. Mark the center of your workspace with a piece of tape as well.

2  Mount the 14'6" ropes onto the dowel using RLHKs, and group them near the center of your workspace.

3  Use RLHKs to mount 18 of the 24' ropes on either side of the shorter ones. Space all of the RLHKs evenly across your workspace.

## KNOTTING

4  Work 1 row of 2 SKs. If you're using an irregularly shaped object like a branch or piece of driftwood, it is more important that this row be level than that it hug the edge of the branch all the way across.

5  Work an alternating row of 2 SKs. From this point on, the curtain will be divided at the center. You may find it helpful to mark the centermost SK with a piece of tape (or a safety pin) as a reminder until the division is established.

6  Work another 3 alternating rows of 2 SKs each, maintaining the gap at the center of the piece. [A]

7  Using the leftmost 4 cords, work a column as follows: 2½" below, work a 20" sinnet of SKs, and then work 2 SKs 2½" below that.

8  Several inches below, work an OK in each of the column's two working cords. These knots do not need to be at exactly the same height. Trim the working cords 12" below the lowest SK, and unravel them below the OKs. Do not trim the filler cords yet.

9  Using the rightmost 4 cords, work a column as follows: 1 SK 2½" below, and then, 2½" below that, work a 16" sinnet of SKs (about 23 SKs in total); then work 2 SKs 2½" below those. The bottom knot of the right- and left-hand columns should line up horizontally. If they don't, take a moment to adjust your knotting.

10  Repeat step 8, this time trimming the working cords 15" below the lowest SK above them. Again, do not trim the filler cords yet. Ignore the cords making up both of the columns that you've just worked in the remaining knotting instructions.

11  Next, 2½" below the alternating rows of 2 SKs, use the cords held double to work a row of SKs. [B]

12  With the cords still held double, work another 3 SKs in sequence beneath each of the outermost 2 SKs on either side of the previous row, spacing them 5" apart.

## WINGS

13  Complete the following rows using the 64 centermost cords. Be sure to maintain the division at the center of the curtain as you work.

Row 1: 2½" below, work a row of 2 SKs.

Row 2: Skip 2 cords, work 7 sinnets of 2 SKs, skip 4 cords, work 7 sinnets of 2 SKs, skip 2 cords.

Row 3: Skip 4 cords, work 14 sinnets of 2 SKs, skip 4 cords.

Row 4: Skip 6 cords, work 6 sinnets of 2 SKs, skip 4 cords, work 6 sinnets of 2 SKs, skip 6 cords.

Row 5: Skip 8 cords, work 12 sinnets of 2 SKs, skip 8 cords.

CONTINUED

Row 6: Skip 10 cords, work 5 sinnets of 2 SKs, skip 4 cords, work 5 sinnets of 2 SKs, skip 10 cords.

Row 7: Skip 16 cords, work 8 sinnets of 2 SKs, skip 16 cords.

Row 8: Skip 22 cords, work 2 sinnets of 2 SKs, skip 4 cords, work 2 sinnets of 2 SKs, skip 22 cords.

Row 9: Work 1 SK with the first 8 cords held double, skip 20 cords, work 2 sinnets of 2 SKs, skip 20 cords, and then work 1 SK with the last 8 cords held double.

Row 10: Next, 5" below, use the first 16 cords to work 2 SKs in a row with the cords held double. Then, work an OK in each of the next 32 cords. Use the last 16 cords to work 2 SKs in a row with the cords held double. [C]

## LEGS

14 Complete the following rows once on either side, using the outermost 18 cords.

Rows 1–3: 2½" below, work 3 alternating rows of 2 SKs.

Row 4: Then, 2½" below, work a row of SKs with the cords held double.

Row 5: Next, 5" below, work a row of SKs with the cords held double.

Row 6: Repeat Row 5.

Rows 7–9: Repeat Rows 1–3.

Row 10: Now, 7" below, work a row of OKs. Include the filler cords from the columns you worked in steps 7–10 in this row. As you can see, these OKs do not need to line up perfectly. Letting a few knots stray here adds interest and makes your piece unique. [D]

## FINISHING

15 Trim the centermost 32 cords about 7" below the OKs, in line with the adjacent SK pattern.

16 Trim the cords at the bottom of the legs as well as the filler cords from the two outer columns 12" below the OKs.

17 Unravel all of the ends to create fringe, and remove any remaining tape.

# SISTERS OF THE MOON WALL HANGING +++

Light streaming through detailed knotwork adds ambience and magic to a room. I designed this large curtain panel with that in mind, leaving lots of negative space both to highlight the diamonds and make them shine. Whether your goal is to add flair to your shower, make a breezy room divider, or put a statement wall piece above your bed, this versatile project will get you there. Or simply place a pair of these over large front windows and let some morning sun shimmer through.

**FINISHED SIZE**
6' wide by 5' long, plus fringe

**KNOTS & TECHNIQUES**
Reverse Lark's Head Knot (RLHK), page 23

Square Knot (SK), page 25

Alternating Square Knots (ASK), page 28

Alternating Rows of Square Knots, page 29

Vertical Double Half Hitch (VDHH), page 30

Overhand Knot (OK), page 33

Bundling, page 33

**SUGGESTED SETUP**
Supported Dowel or Hanging Dowel, page 18*

**SUPPLIES**
1,793' white cotton rope (5mm diameter)

13' scrap rope

Washi or masking tape

144 rubber bands

**CUT LIST**
One 45' length white cotton rope

Seventy-two 24' lengths white cotton rope

One 20' length white cotton rope

Thirteen 1' lengths scrap rope

*Given the large amount of rope involved in this project, it is especially important to use a sturdy dowel that can safely support twice the weight of the rope you will be using.

CONTINUED

## PREPARATION

1 Bundle all of the 24' ropes with the rubber bands.

2 Fold the 45' rope up into just one bundle, leaving a tail of about 12'.

3 Tape off a 6' wide workspace on the dowel.

4 Measure 7' from one end of the 20' rope, and mark this point with tape. Repeat at the other end. This rope will be your mounting cord, and you will mount your knotting ropes onto the 6' of rope between its two taped points.

5 Line up one piece of tape on the mounting cord with one of those on the dowel. Using a piece of scrap rope, tie the mounting cord securely to the underside of the dowel at this point.

6 Mount six of the 24' ropes onto the mounting cord using RLHKs; then tie the mounting cord to the dowel with another piece of scrap rope. Repeat this process until all seventy-two 24' ropes have been mounted.

7 Arrange the RLHKs so that they are spaced evenly across the 6' workspace, making sure that the taped points on the mounting cord line up with those on the dowel. The scrap rope ties should end up about 6" apart. [A]

## KNOTTING

8 Work 5 rows of ASKs, leaving ½" between knots.

9 Leaving a 6'-long tail, use the 45' rope to work 1 row of VDHHs from left to right, working each knot around 2 cords at a time. Be careful not to place your knots too close together. Space them so that the overall width of the piece is maintained. [B]

10 Work the Diamond Panel (see facing page).

11 Then, 4" below, work 14 rows of ASKs, leaving ½" between the knots.

## FINISHING

12 Trim all 72 cords used in the knotting pattern to about 6" (or longer, if desired) and unravel them.

13 Tie an OK in line with the lowest row of ASKs in each end of the mounting cord and each end of the cord around which you worked the row of VDHHs. Trim each cord to match the length of the fringe, and unravel it below the OK to make a decorative tassel.

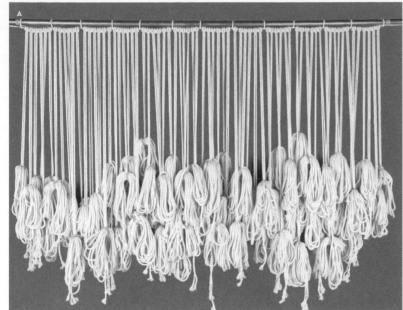

## DIAMOND PANEL

Because this panel has bilateral symmetry, the method for completing each row will only be described from the left edge to the center. To work the entire row, simply complete the left side, work the central SK (where noted), and then follow the instructions for the left side once again in reverse.

• Use the following row-by-row instructions along with the photograph on page 109 to complete.

• Work all rows ½" apart.

• Do not include the tail ends of the mounting cord or those of the working cord used to make the row of VDHHs in the knotting of the Diamond Panel or the ASKs below it. To avoid accidentally incorporating these cords, you may wish to loop them around the dowel or otherwise secure them up and out of the way until they are needed in step 13.

• Given the large amounts of negative space in this panel, it is easy for cords to become wrapped around each other. Take a moment to ensure that the cords are in the correct order and have not become twisted before working each knot.

Row 1: 2½" below, skip 16 cords, SK, skip 20 cords, SK, skip 26 cords. Work an SK in the center, then repeat the previous instructions in reverse.

Row 2: Skip 14 cords, work 2 SKs, skip 16 cords, work 2 SKs, skip 22 cords, SK. Repeat in reverse.

Row 3: Skip 12 cords, SK, skip 4 cords, SK, skip 12 cords, SK, skip 4 cords, SK, skip 18 cords, SK, skip 2 cords. Repeat in reverse.

Row 4: Skip 10 cords, SK, skip 8 cords, SK, skip 12 cords, work 2 SKs, skip 18 cords, SK, skip 4 cords. Repeat in reverse.

Row 5: Skip 8 cords, SK, skip 4 cords, SK, skip 4 cords, SK, skip 12 cords, SK, skip 18 cords, SK, skip 6 cords. Repeat in reverse.

Row 6: Skip 6 cords, SK, skip 16 cords, SK, skip 30 cords, SK, skip 8 cords. Repeat in reverse.

Row 7: Skip 4 cords, SK, skip 20 cords, SK, skip 26 cords, SK, skip 10 cords. Repeat in reverse.

CONTINUED

Row 8: Skip 2 cords, SK, skip 4 cords, SK, skip 8 cords, SK, skip 4 cords, SK, skip 6 cords, SK, skip 12 cords, SK, skip 10 cords. Work an SK in the center, then repeat the previous instructions in reverse.

Row 9: Skip 4 cords, SK, skip 20 cords, SK, skip 22 cords, SK, skip 14 cords. Repeat in reverse.

Row 10: Skip 6 cords, SK, skip 16 cords, SK, skip 22 cords, SK, skip 16 cords. Repeat in reverse.

Row 11: Skip 8 cords, SK, skip 4 cords, SK, skip 4 cords, SK, skip 22 cords, SK, skip 14 cords, SK. Repeat in reverse.

Row 12: Skip 10 cords, SK, skip 8 cords, SK, skip 22 cords, SK, skip 20 cords. Repeat in reverse.

Row 13: Skip 12 cords, SK, skip 4 cords, SK, skip 22 cords, SK, skip 8 cords, SK, skip 10 cords. Repeat in reverse.

Row 14: Skip 14 cords, work 2 SKs, skip 26 cords, SK, skip 20 cords. Repeat in reverse.

Row 15: SK, skip 12 cords, SK, skip 12 cords, SK, skip 14 cords, SK, skip 18 cords, SK. Repeat in reverse.

Row 16: Skip 52 cords, SK, skip 16 cords. Repeat in reverse.

Row 17: Skip 16 cords, SK, skip 20 cords, SK, skip 10 cords, SK, skip 14 cords. Repeat in reverse.

Row 18: Skip 14 cords, work 2 SKs, skip 34 cords, SK, skip 10 cords. Work an SK in the center, then repeat the previous instructions in reverse.

Row 19: Skip 12 cords, SK, skip 4 cords, SK, skip 34 cords, SK, skip 10 cords. Repeat in reverse.

Row 20: Skip 14 cords, work 2 SKs, skip 38 cords, SK, skip 8 cords. Repeat in reverse.

Row 21: Skip 16 cords, SK, skip 20 cords, SK, skip 18 cords, SK, skip 6 cords. Repeat in reverse.

Row 22: Skip 38 cords, work 2 SKs, skip 18 cords, SK, skip 4 cords. Repeat in reverse.

Row 23: Skip 36 cords, SK, skip 4 cords, SK, skip 18 cords, SK, skip 2 cords. Repeat in reverse.

Row 24: Skip 34 cords, SK, skip 8 cords, SK, skip 18 cords, SK. Repeat in reverse.

Row 25: Skip 36 cords, SK, skip 4 cords, SK, skip 22 cords. Work an SK in the center, then repeat the previous instructions in reverse.

Row 26: Skip 38 cords, work 2 SKs, skip 26 cords. Repeat in reverse.

Row 27: Skip 40 cords, SK, skip 28 cords. Repeat in reverse.

Row 28: 1½" below, skip 16 cords, SK, skip 50 cords. Work an SK in the center, then repeat the previous instructions in reverse.

Row 29: Skip 14 cords, work 2 SKs, skip 46 cords, SK. Repeat in reverse.

Row 30: Skip 12 cords, SK, skip 4 cords, SK, skip 42 cords, SK, skip 2 cords. Repeat in reverse.

Row 31: SK, skip 6 cords, SK, skip 8 cords, SK, skip 14 cords, SK, skip 24 cords, SK. Repeat in reverse.

Row 32: Skip 12 cords, SK, skip 4 cords, SK, skip 46 cords. Work an SK in the center, then repeat the previous instructions in reverse.

Row 33: Skip 14 cords, work 2 SKs, skip 50 cords. Repeat in reverse.

Row 34: Skip 16 cords, SK, skip 52 cords. Repeat in reverse.

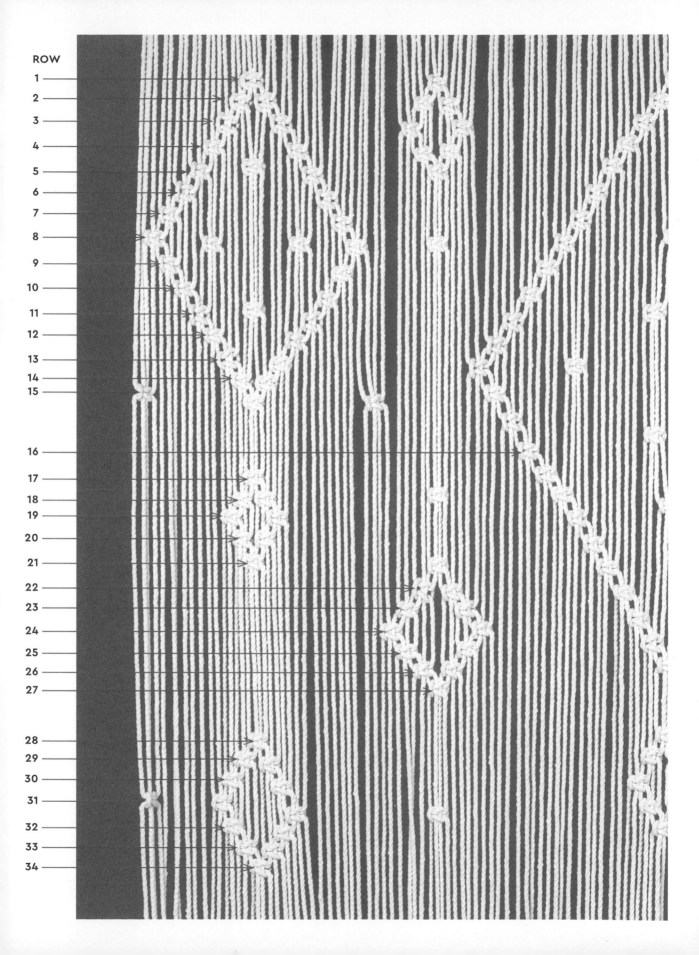

ROW

1
2
3
4
5
6
7
8
9
10
11
12
13
14
15

16
17
18
19
20
21
22
23
24
25
26
27

28
29
30
31
32
33
34

# I AM NOT DREAMING TENT +++

When I was a little girl, I dreamed of sleeping under a gauzy canopy, surrounded by plants. Set up in a large bedroom, this macramé tent would be a whimsical place to lounge. Amid a mountainside of blooming wildflowers, it could be the centerpiece of a modern boho wedding scene.

My original frame came from a vintage hunting tent, but newer modern versions can be purchased, too. (See Resources, page 240.) And although it looks complex, the knotwork of this tent consists only of alternating square knots made in panels.

**FINISHED SIZE**
8' long by 8' wide, 5' side-wall height, 8' height at tallest point

**KNOTS & TECHNIQUES**
Lark's Head Knot (LHK), page 23

Square Knot (SK), page 25

Sinnet of Square Knots, page 27

Alternating Square Knots (ASK), page 28

Alternating Rows of Square Knots, page 29

Overhand Knot (OK), page 33

**SUPPLIES**
6,168' white cotton rope (5mm diameter)

Wall tent frame

**CUT LIST**
Two 40' lengths

Twenty 35' lengths

Eighty-four 30' lengths

Twenty-four 32' lengths

Eighty-four 25' lengths

CONTINUED

## PREPARATION

1 Fold all the ropes in half and organize by length. Since you'll be working with several similar lengths of the same rope, be sure to note the length of each set of ropes in some way.

## SIDE WALLS

2 Mount forty-two 25' ropes onto the horizontal bar at the top of one side of the tent frame using LHKs.

3 Space the LHKs out evenly in pairs, leaving about 2" of space at the far left and right ends of the pole.

4 Then, 2" below, work a row of SKs.

5 Work 17 rows of ASKs, 2½" apart. [A]

6 Then, 2½" below, work an alternating row of 4 SKs.

7 Trim all cords to 7", or 1–2" above the floor, and unravel. [B]

8 Repeat steps 2–7 on the other side of the tent.

## BACK

9 Work the following rows to complete the upper, triangular section of the back of the tent. Work all ASKs 2½" apart. [C]

Row 1: Facing the back of the tent from the outside, mount one 35' rope onto each angled pole 1½" from the apex using an LHK. Use the 4 resulting cords to work an SK 3" below the apex. Then mount a pair of 35' ropes side by side 2½" farther down each angled pole using LHKs, and work an SK right up against the pole with the 4 cords extending from each pair. Line up the 3 knots you've worked so far to form a horizontal row of 3 SKs.

Row 2: Next, 2½" farther down the angled pole on the right, mount a 35' rope using an

LHK. Combine the newly mounted cords with the two to their left, and work an SK 1" from the LHK and 2½" from the SK above. Repeat on the left, then work SKs with the remaining cords to form a complete row of ASKs.

Row 3: Then, 2½" farther down the angled pole on the right, mount a 35' rope using an LHK. Combine the newly mounted cords with the two to their left, and work an SK 1¾" from the LHK and 2½" from the SK above. Repeat on the left; then work SKs with the remaining cords to complete the row of ASKs.

Row 4: Mount a 35' rope as you did in Rows 2–3, combine its cords with the two to their left, and work an SK 2½" from both the LHK and the SK above. Then mount another two 35' ropes using LHKs 2½" farther down the pole, and use their cords to work an SK right next to the pole. Repeat on the left and work SKs with the remaining cords to complete the row of ASKs.

Rows 5–10: Repeat Rows 2–4 twice more, switching to 32' ropes once you have used up your 35' ropes.

Rows 11–12: Repeat Rows 2–3.

Row 13: 2½" farther down the angled pole on the right, mount a 32' rope using an LHK. Use its cords and the two to their left to work an SK 2½" from both the LHK and the SK above. Repeat on the left and complete the row of ASKs.

Row 14: Mount another 32' rope 2½" farther down the pole on the right using an LHK, and use its cords along with the next two to their left to work an SK 3" from the pole and 2½" from the SK above. Repeat on the left and complete the row of ASKs. [D]

10 Work 19 rows of ASKs, spacing the knots 2½" apart.

11 Repeat steps 6–7 of the side walls.

CONTINUED

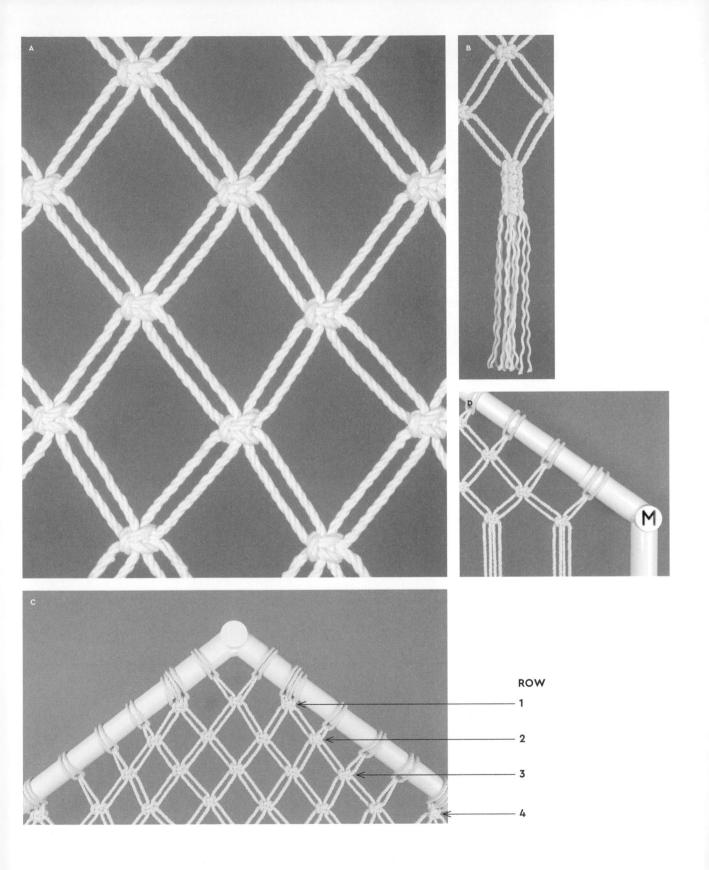

ROW

1

2

3

4

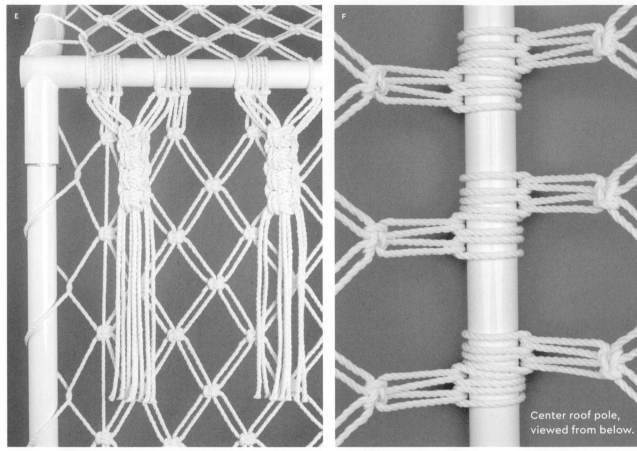

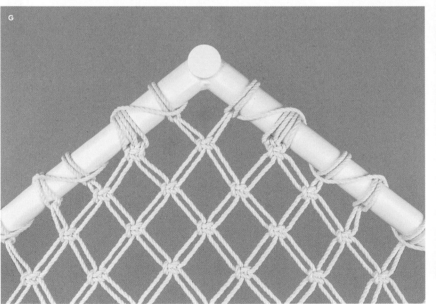

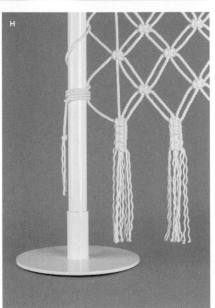

Center roof pole,
viewed from below.

## ROOF

**12** Facing the inside of the left side wall, mount forty-two 30' ropes onto the pole at the top of the tent using LHKs.

**13** Space the LHKs evenly across the pole in pairs, leaving 2" free at either end.

**14** Then, 2½" below, work a row of SKs.

**15** Work 20 rows of ASKs, spacing the knots 2½" apart.

**16** Next, secure the roof panel to the pole at the top of the side wall using SKs. Lay the cords of the roof panel over the bar at the top of the right side wall. Face the right side wall from the outside of the tent and pull the SK in the lower left corner of the roof panel down diagonally to the left until it rests against the top of the horizontal pole at the top of the side wall, just to the left of the leftmost LHK. Use the cords of this SK to knot around the pole by bringing the filler cords below the pole and working an SK using all four of its cords. Then, pull the filler cords down and toward you to tighten the knot and position it on the underside of the pole.

**17** Knot all of the remaining cords of the roof panel around the pole as you did in step 16, placing the new SKs between the pairs of LHKs at the top of the side wall.

**18** Working from left to right with the cords held double, work 10 sinnets of 4 SKs 2" below. [E] You should have 4 cords remaining at the far right (rear) of the roof panel. Use these cords to work the following column: 4 SKs and then 3 SKs 4" below them.

**19** Trim all the cords 9" below the knotting.

**20** Use LHKs to mount the remaining forty-two 30' ropes onto the pole at the top of the tent in pairs between the existing knotting. Space them 2" apart. [F]

**21** Repeat steps 14–19 on the other side, using the newly mounted cords.

## FINISHING

**22** Fold one of the 40' ropes in half, and wrap its center around the back end of the pole at the top of the tent.

**23** Bring the cord on the right under and around the angled pole on the right. Then bring it down through the first hole at the edge of the roof panel's knotting, and under and around the pole again. Pull tight.

**24** Repeat step 23 down the edge of the roof panel until you reach the top of the side wall so that the entire back edge of the roof panel is secured to the angled pole. [G]

**25** Continue down the side wall, wrapping in the same manner, *except* this time bring the wrapping cord *between* the two cords at the edge of the side panel each time.

**26** When you reach the bottom, tightly wrap the cord around the pole several times, and secure it with an OK.

**27** Tie another OK about 5" below, and trim the cord 5" below that.

**28** Unravel the cords. [H]

**29** Repeat steps 23–28 on the left side.

**30** Repeat steps 22–29 in the back of the tent.

# LIGHTING

Lighting makes all the difference, and since modern life doesn't come to a halt when the sun goes down, we have to make our own. How best to cast light upon our space is one of the most critical decisions we face when arranging a room. It's the difference between a space that draws us in and one that we can't wait to leave, between a productive zone and one of eyestrain and frustration. A well-chosen lamp or fixture does double duty—both enhancing the look of its surroundings and accommodating the activities therein.

Paired with the right bulb, the DNA Cord Light is great for reading and would be ideal beside your favorite chair or as a bedside lamp. The Breeze Block Lamp is versatile, serving either as the shade of a floor lamp or as a pendant hung from the ceiling. The Dancing Shadows Lantern doesn't actually need to be a lamp at all, working equally well as a textural hanging or an ornament in a lonely corner. The same applies to the Cloud Bursting Lantern, which can look fantastic over a dining table, either as party decoration or for everyday celebrating.

SAFETY NOTE: Be sure to choose a lightbulb that is safe for use inside of macramé pieces. I recommend using only LED lights inside your macramé, as they produce little heat.

Whether your vibe is modern, classic, artsy, or sophisticated, the DNA Cord Light (page 122), Breeze Block Lamp (page 131), and Cloud Bursting Lantern (page 134), lend a unique touch to any style of décor.

# DNA CORD LIGHT +

The technique of knotting a spiral around a cord or cable can be used in a variety of ways. From light cords to computer cords to phone chargers to speaker cables, if you can't hide them, flaunt them—and your knotting skills!

This pattern is written for a light cord but can easily be adapted for any type or length of cord or cable. If you are using the 6mm hemp rope suggested in the pattern, simply measure the cord you would like to cover and allow 11' of rope per foot of cord length. If you'd like to use a different material, make a swatch (see page 34) to find out how much rope you will need.

There are a couple of ways you can set up to make this project. Choose the one that works for you. One simple option is to find a comfortable chair and hold the light cord between your knees as you knot around it. Alternatively, tie a piece of scrap rope beneath the socket of the light cord and secure it to a C-clamp setup. If you choose this method, I recommend using a swivel clip so that you can rotate your work easily as the knotting spirals.

---

**FINISHED SIZE**
15' long

**KNOTS & TECHNIQUES**
Half Square Knot (HSK), page 24

Square Knot (SK), page 25

Mounting with a Half Square Knot (HSK), see page 26

Sinnet of Square Knots, page 27

Half Square Knot Spiral, page 27

Bundling, page 33

**SUGGESTED SETUP**
C-Clamp, page 18

**SUPPLIES**
164' hemp rope in black (6mm diameter)

15' pendant-light cord set

Scrap rope (optional)

S-hook (optional)

Swivel clip (optional)

2 rubber bands

12mm plastic or metal crochet hook (optional)

---

## PREPARATION

1 Bundle the 164' rope with the rubber bands.

## KNOTTING

2 Mount the 164' rope onto the light cord just below the base of the socket using an HSK.

3 Work a spiral of HSKs around the light cord, stopping only once you've reached the switch and spacing your knots so that you have about 24 HSKs per foot. To avoid running out of rope before you are finished, be sure to maintain consistent knot spacing as you work. Take a minute to measure and count your knots periodically. [A]

4 Securely work an SK around the light cord directly below the switch. [B]

5 Continue working SKs until about 6" of the electric cord remains. [C]

6 Leaving a gap, work your next SK just below the base of the plug. [D]

7 Continue to work SKs until the gap is filled in. [E]

## FINISHING

8 Trim the ends to 3" and either unravel them and let them hang out, or use a crochet hook to hide them within the knotting.

# DANCING SHADOWS LANTERN ++

For three weeks in 2009, I meandered through northern Thailand, eating spicy food, getting massages, and eyeing all the textiles. On one of my first few days in Chiang Mai, I found a pair of two-tiered cotton lanterns adorned with tassels at a local market. Though I still had weeks of travel ahead of me, and only a backpack to store my discoveries, I bought them anyway.

Those treasures were the inspiration for this multitiered macramé lantern. Like the ones I found in Thailand, this lantern packs fairly flat for travel, in case you decide to bring one along to decorate a wedding or garden party, or to leave as a gift when visiting a distant friend.

**FINISHED SIZE**
4' long by 10" diameter

**KNOTS & TECHNIQUES**
Reverse Lark's Head Knot (RLHK), page 23

Square Knot (SK), page 25

Sinnet of Square Knots, page 27

Alternating Square Knots (ASK), page 28

Alternating Rounds of Square Knots, page 29

Alternating Rows/Rounds of Two (or More) Square Knots, page 29

Overhand Knot (OK), page 33

**SUGGESTED SETUP**
Hook, page 18

**SUPPLIES**
497' white cotton rope (5mm diameter)

1¼" brass triangle or ring

Two 10" brass hoops

8" brass hoop

6" brass hoop

Washi or masking tape

S-hook (optional)

Swivel clip (optional)

Light cord and LED bulb (optional)

**CUT LIST**
One 17' length

Forty-eight 10' lengths

CONTINUED

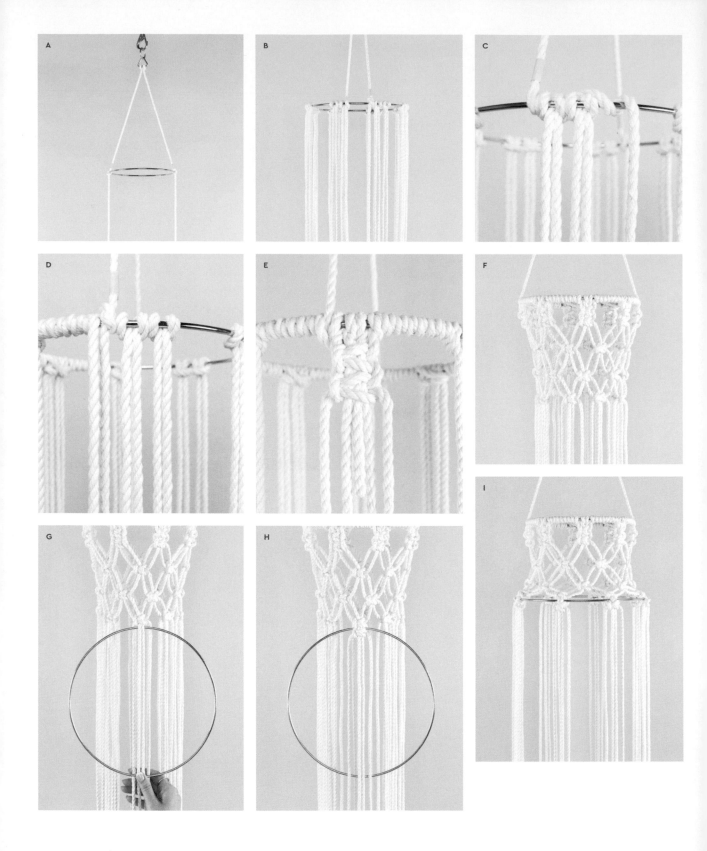

## PREPARATION

1  Mount the 17' rope onto the 1¼" brass triangle or ring using an RLHK and hang it from a S-hook, using a swivel clip, if desired.

2  Measure 12" down each cord from the base of the knot and mark this point with tape.

3  Just below the tape, tie each cord securely onto the 8" hoop using an OK. Position the 2 OKs opposite each other so that the hoop hangs horizontally. [A]

## TOP TIER

4  Using RLHKs, mount two 10' ropes onto the hoop directly to the right of each OK.

5  Then, using RLHKs, mount 3 pairs of 10' ropes onto each side of the hoop, spacing them evenly. [B]

6  Untie one of the OKs while maintaining the tape's position relative to the hoop, bring the cord behind the 2 RLHKs to its right, and wrap it around the hoop. [C]

7  Wrap the cord tightly around the hoop another six times; then bring it behind the next pair of RLHKs and back around to the front as you did in step 6. Continue in this way, wrapping the cord around the hoop and behind each pair of RLHKs, until half of the hoop is covered and you have reached the other OK. [D]

8  Repeat steps 6–7 on the opposite side so that the entire hoop is covered.

9  Bring one of the wrapping cords behind the 2 cords to its right so that it hangs in the center of the group of 4 cords next to it. To secure the end of the wrapping cord, use these cords to work a sinnet of 2 SKs, holding the wrapping cord at the center as a third filler cord. [E]

10  Cut the wrapping cord just below the SKs.

11  Repeat steps 9–10 on the opposite side.

12  Work a sinnet of 2 SKs with each of the remaining groups of 4 hanging cords so that you have a complete round of 2 SKs.

13  Work 3 rounds of ASKs, leaving 1½" between knots. [F]

## SECOND TIER

14  Hold a 10" hoop so that its edge rests just below an SK from the previous round. Mount the cords onto the hoop by bringing the filler cords to the front [G] and working an SK [H].

15  Repeat step 14 using the group of 4 cords directly opposite to hang the hoop in a horizontal position. Then repeat all the way around. [I]

CONTINUED

16 Cover the hoop all the way around by mounting four 10' ropes in each gap left by the previous knotting using RLHKs.

17 Work SKs using the newly mounted ropes so that you have a complete round of SKs beneath the hoop. [J]

18 Work 2 alternating rounds of 2 SKs.

19 Then, 4" below, work a round of 2 SKs.

20 Work an alternating round of 2 SKs. [K]

## THIRD TIER (UPPER)

21 Rest the edge of the second 10" hoop just below and in between 2 SKs from the previous round. This time, mount the cords onto the hoop using alternating SKs. To do so, bring the rightmost cord of the SK on the left and the leftmost cord of the SK on the right in front of the hoop. [L]

22 Work an SK, using the 2 cords in front of the hoop as filler cords and those directly to their right and left as working cords. Repeat with the cords directly opposite, and then with those remaining, securing the hoop in a horizontal position. [M]

23 Pick up the rightmost 2 cords of any SK along with the 6 cords directly to their right. Now, 1" below the previous round, work an SK using the left- and rightmost cords of this group as working cords, and the remaining 6 cords as filler. [N]

24 Repeat step 23 all the way around.

25 Select 4 of the longest filler cords from one of the SKs in the previous round. Use these to work an SK 2" below the previous round. Repeat all the way around. Secure any cords you did not work in this round up and out of the way. [O]

## THIRD TIER (INNER)

26 Attach the 6" hoop using the method detailed in steps 21–22.

27 Work 2 rounds of ASKs.

28 Trim the ends of the cords extending from this tier to 14" and unravel. [P] Don't worry if a few cords are already shorter than 14"; subtle imperfections like this will make your piece all the more beautiful and unique!

## THIRD TIER (OUTER)

29 Pull down the cords you set aside in step 25. Use these cords to work 2 rounds of ASKs, leaving about 2" between knots.

30 Trim the ends of the cords extending from this tier to 6" and unravel them. [Q]

## FINISHING

31 Hang the lantern as desired, using hardware intended for your ceiling type and that can safely support your lantern's weight. [R] If using a light cord, drop it in through the top of the lantern, centering the bulb in the middle of the second tier.

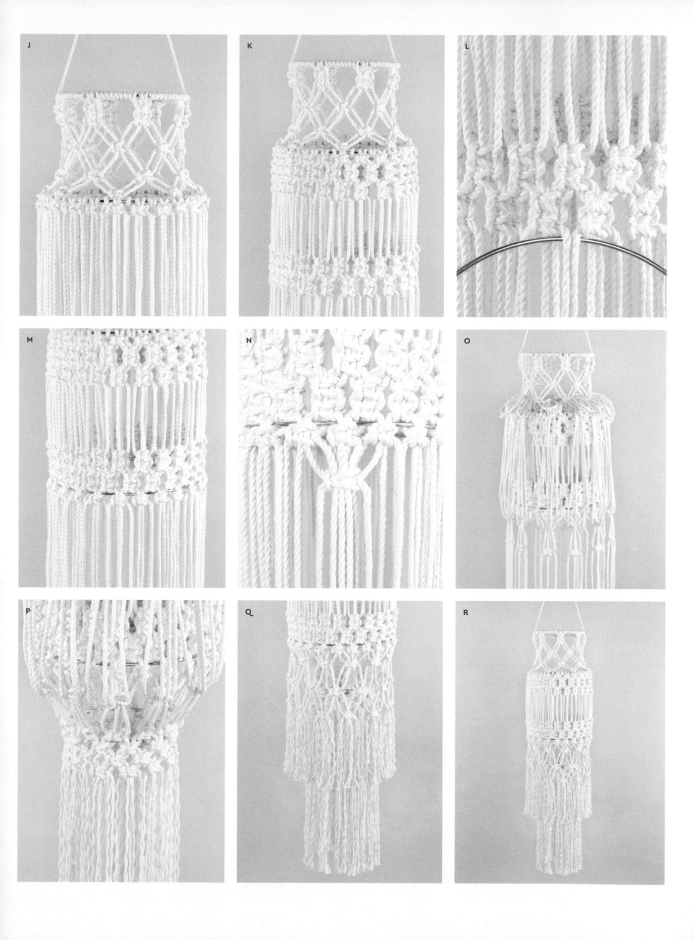

# BREEZE BLOCK LAMP ++

The circular shapes of modernist Palm Springs breeze blocks catch my eye whenever I see them. Their geometry, breaking the light that flows through them into patterned shadows, inspired this lamp shade. I imagine similar, delightful shadows cast through the spatial knotwork when perched atop a tall floor lamp, as pictured. A pair would look great flanking a bed or set against a deeply colored backdrop.

**FINISHED SIZE**
19" long, including fringe, by 18" diameter

**KNOTS & TECHNIQUES**
Reverse Lark's Head Knot (RLHK), page 23

Square Knot (SK), page 25

Sinnet of Square Knots, page 27

Alternating Square Knots (ASK), page 28

Alternating Rounds of Square Knots, page 29

Alternating Rows/Rounds of Two (or More) Square Knots, page 29

Horizontal Double Half Hitch (HDHH), page 30

Overhand Knot (OK), page 33

**SUGGESTED SETUP**
Hook, page 18

**SUPPLIES**
492' white cotton rope (5mm diameter)

24' scrap rope or string

18"-diameter lamp-shade spider*

Swivel clip (optional)

Lamp base or light cord

LED bulb

**CUT LIST**
Forty 10' lengths white cotton rope

Two 6' lengths white cotton rope

Forty 2' lengths white cotton rope

Four 6' lengths scrap rope

*If you plan to place this shade on a lamp base, be sure to select a spider that is compatible with the base you'd like to use.

CONTINUED

LIGHTING

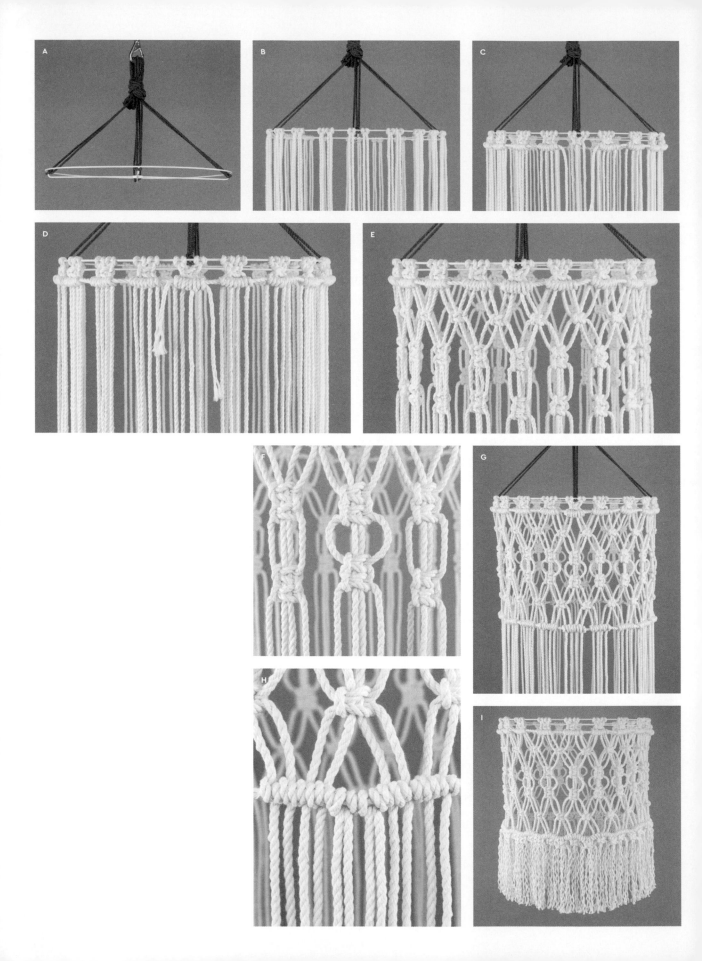

## PREPARATION

1 Tie the center of each length of scrap rope to the end of one of the spokes of the spider using an OK.

2 Bring the ends of the 4 scrap ropes together over the center of the spider, and tie them all together in a slipknot. Hang the loop of the slipknot from the S-hook, and swivel clip, if using. [A]

3 Mount ten of the 10' lengths onto each quadrant of the hoop using RLHKs. Slide one knot to either side of each spoke, and space the rest evenly in pairs. [B]

## KNOTTING

4 Work 1 round of SKs.

5 Pick up a 6' rope to use as a filler cord for the following round: leaving a 5" tail, work HDHHs in evenly spaced groups of four until only 4 cords remain. [C]

6 Work the last 4 HDHHs in the round securely around both ends of the mounting cord. [D]

7 Adjust the knotting as necessary so that the circumference of the round matches that of the spider as closely as possible. Once you are happy with the spacing, tie the ends of the filler cord together (out of sight behind the last group of HDHHs you worked) using 2 OKs. Trim the ends of the filler cord to ½".

8 Next, 1½" below, work a round of SKs that alternate with the groups of HDHHs above them. (In other words, each SK you work in this round should sit below and between two groups of knots in the row above it.)

9 Now, 1½" below, work an alternating round of 2 SKs.

10 Then, 1½" below, work a round of 2 SKs. [E]

11 Pick up any 2 SK sinnet from the previous round and slide it up ½" along its filler cords. Repeat all the way around. [F]

12 Now, 1½" below, work a round of ASKs.

13 Then, 1½" below, use the remaining 6' rope to repeat steps 5–7, this time, working an alternating round. In other words, knot the groups of 4 HDHHs *between* the SKs in the round above them so that the cords between the 2 rounds extend down diagonally. [G]

14 Using RLHKs, mount two 2' ropes onto the mounting cord in each empty space. [H]

15 Work a round of SKs.

## FINISHING

16 Trim all cords to 6" and unravel them. [I]

17 Remove the scrap rope, and complete with your chosen light cord or lamp base and bulb.

# CLOUD BURSTING LANTERN +++

This lantern's, simple shape illuminates a web of intriguing complexity, its layers suggesting both depth and spaciousness. I first made it for a pop-up show at Poketo, a shop in Los Angeles where I've often held workshops. It hung beside two other lanterns of similar size, each hovering at a different height over a pattern-filled seating area. Lanterns of all kinds look good in groups, but this one, centered over a dining table, can be a knockout on its own.

**FINISHED SIZE**
18" diameter by 36" long, from top of ring to bottom of fringe

**KNOTS & TECHNIQUES**
Reverse Lark's Head Knot (RLHK), page 23

Square Knot (SK), page 25

Sinnet of Square Knots, page 27

Alternating Square Knots (ASK), page 28

Alternating Rounds of Square Knots, page 29

Overhand Knot (OK), page 33

**SUGGESTED SETUP**
Hook, page 18

**SUPPLIES**
780' white cotton rope (5mm diameter)

3" brass ring

18" white metal hoop

18" brass hoop

Two 12" white metal hoops

Washi or masking tape

Swivel clip (optional)

Light cord and LED bulb (optional)

**CUT LIST**
Fifty 14' lengths

Two 40" lengths

CONTINUED

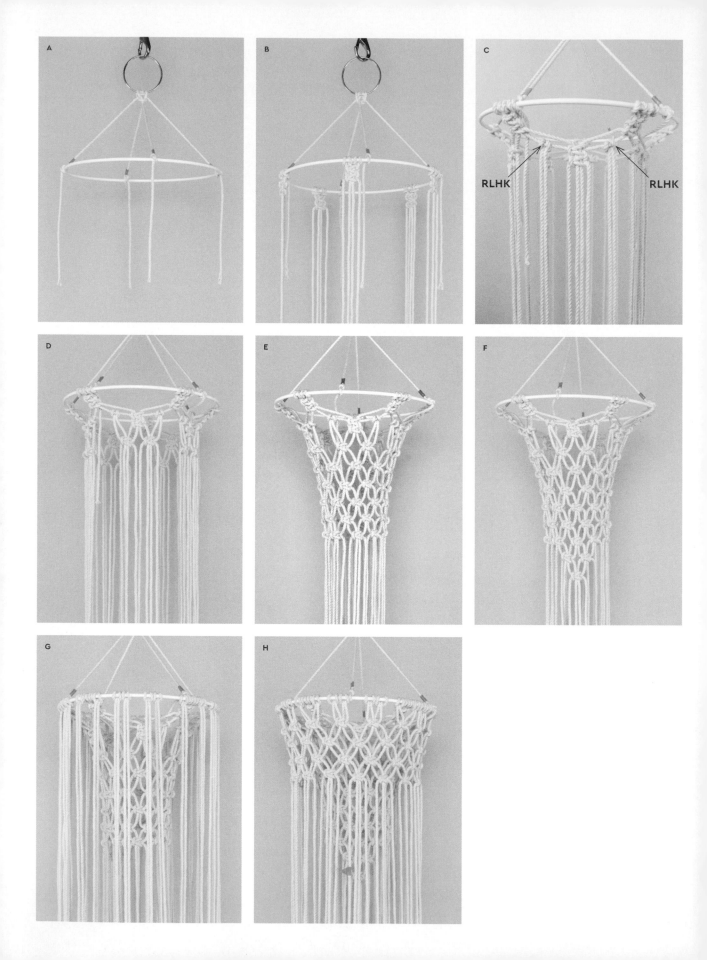

## PREPARATION

1  Mount a 40" rope onto the 3" brass ring using an RLHK, and hang it from a hook, using a swivel clip, if desired.

2  Measure 7" down each cord from the base of the knot and mark this point with tape.

3  Just below the tape, tie each cord securely onto the 12" hoop using 2 OKs. Position the 2 pairs of OKs opposite each other so that the hoop hangs horizontally.

4  Use an RLHK to mount the second 40" rope over the RLHK of the first, and repeat steps 2–3 with the cords extending from it.

5  Position the 4 OKs so that they divide the hoop into four equal parts. [A]

## TOP TIER (INNER)

6  Mount ten 14' ropes onto the hoop and space them evenly in pairs.

7  Work a round of 2 SKs. [B]

8  Leaving 2" between knots, work an alternating round of 2 SKs.

9  Using an RLHK, mount a 14' rope onto one of the lower cords running between the first 2 rounds of 2 SKs, centering the RLHK along the cord. Repeat all the way around, for a total of 10 newly mounted ropes. [C]

10  Using the 4 cords extending from any sinnet in the previous round along with the 2 newly mounted cords on either side of them, work 2 SKs in a row, ¾" below. Measure the distance between the new SKs and the sinnet of 2 SKs above them, rather than the RLHKs. Repeat all the way around. [D]

11  Work 5 rounds of ASKs, spacing the knots ¾" apart. [E]

12  Pick any SK from the previous round. Work 2 ASKs ¾" beneath it and then 1 ASK ¾" beneath them, forming a downward-facing point in the knotting. [F]

## TOP TIER (OUTER)

13  Mount thirty 14' ropes onto the hoop using RLHKs, placing 6 ropes in each segment left open by the previous knotting. Slide the first and sixth RLHK in each segment outward so that they rest against the existing knotting. Space the remaining ropes in pairs evenly between them. [G]

14  Then, ¾" below, work a round of SKs.

15  Work 3 rounds of ASKs, spacing the knots ¾" apart.

16  Find an SK in the previous round that is nearly in line with the lowest knot of the inner layer (the one at the bottom of the point). Mark the leftmost cord extending from this knot with a piece of tape, several inches below the previous knotting. Count the taped cord first as you work the following rounds. [H]

Round 1: Beginning with the taped cord, skip 10 cords (including the taped cord) and then work 11 SKs in a row around the back of the lantern, 1" below the previous knotting. After completing these, you should have 6 cords remaining before you come back to the taped cord. Do not work these. The SKs you work in this round should be alternating with those in the round above them.

Round 2: Beginning again with the taped cord, skip 8 cords and then work an SK 1" below. Then, skip to the last 8 cords in the round and work a second SK. Skip the 4 remaining cords.

CONTINUED

Round 3: Next, 1" below, skip 6 cords, work an SK, skip to the last 6 cords in the round, work an SK, then skip 2.

Round 4: Then, 1" below, skip 4 cords, work an SK, skip until 4 cords remain in the round, work an SK. [I]

17 Remove the tape and work 2 ASKs in a row 1" below, in between the knots worked in the previous round.

18 Work an ASK 1" below, in between the two just worked, forming a point. [J]

19 Continue working SKs all the way around the lantern in line with the one at the bottom of the point.

## SECOND TIER

20 Hold the second 12" hoop so that its edge rests just below an SK from the previous round. Mount the hoop onto your project by bringing the working cords to the front and working an SK. [K]

21 Repeat the previous step beneath the SK directly opposite and then with all of those remaining, in order to hang the hoop horizontally.

22 Next, ¾" below, work a round of ASKs. [L]

23 Find the 4 cords extending from the lowest knot of the inner top tier (i.e., the last SK you worked in step 12). Use them, held double, to work an SK around the 4 cords of the lowest SK in front of them. If there is no SK directly in front of them, choose the closest one. [M]

24 Repeat step 23, using the next 4 inner cords to the right as working cords and the 4 cords to the right of the SK that you just completed as filler cords.

25 Repeat again, this time working the next 4 inner cords to the right around the *second* SK to the right in the bottom round. In other words, you will have skipped over one SK in the bottom round without working a knot below it.

26 Repeat steps 24–25 all the way around. When you are finished, you should have worked SKs using all of the inner top tier cords. Make sure that the inner tier is hanging straight before moving on to the next round. If not, take a moment to adjust your knotting. [N]

27 Work 2 ASKs side by side ¾" below each SK you skipped over in the previous round. In line with these knots, work an ASK between each pair of SKs worked in the previous round.

28 Then, 3½" below, work a round of SKs. [O]

## THIRD TIER

29 Mount the white 18" hoop using the same method as in steps 20–21.

30 Work 2 rounds of ASKs, spacing the knots ¾" apart.

31 Mount the 18" brass hoop using the same method as in steps 20–21.

32 Trim all cords to 7" in length. [P]

## FINISHING

33 Untie and remove the 40" rope you added in step 4.

34 Hang the lantern as desired, using hardware intended for your ceiling type and that can support your lantern's weight. [Q]

35 If using, drop the light cord in through the top of the lantern, centering the bulb in the second tier, and install as desired.

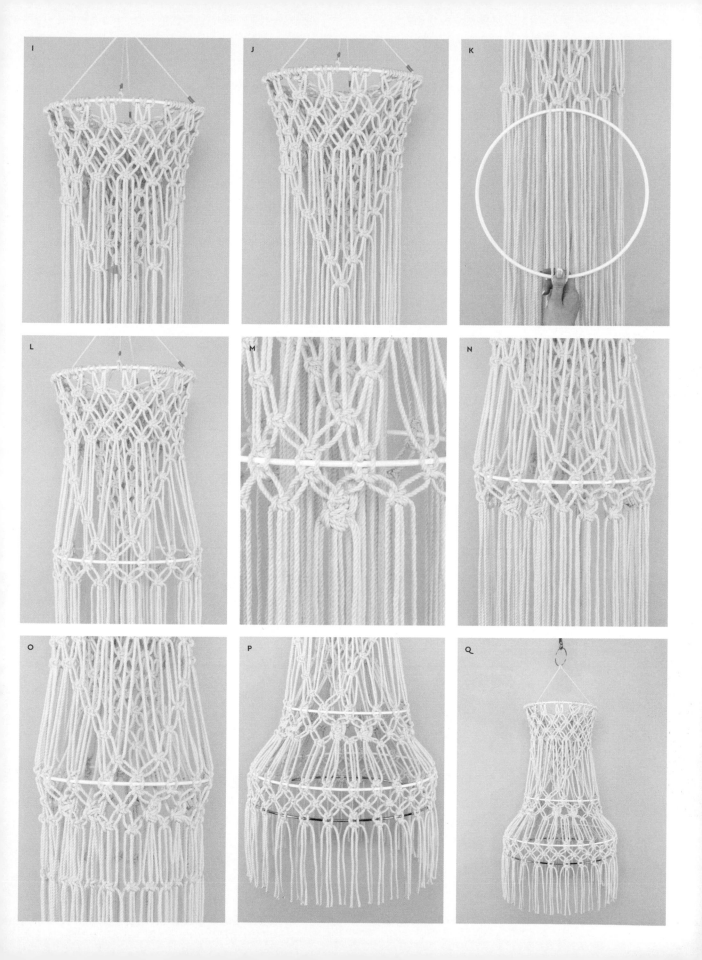

# SEATING

Why make macramé that just sits around when you can make macramé to sit around *on*? Sturdy and unusual, hand-knotted furniture makes a statement—and a beautifully lounge-y one at that. This chapter explores how to spruce up a classic sling-chair frame, reinvent the hoop chair, and get whimsical with a rope swing. You'll also learn how to knot up a daybed, which, surrounded by tropical plants, could turn your living room into a jungle scene reminiscent of a hammock hanging between palm trees, only indoors. Pieces like these are ideal in hot weather, with the space between knots providing cooling airflow. In the winter months, just add a few blankets or sheepskins to cozy them right up!

Above: Romantic arches, walls painted a sumptuous blue, and a 1960s handmade-glass light fixture paired with the Hoop Chair (page 157) create a playful and unexpected corner lounge.

Opposite: A pair of Summer Sling Chairs (page 151) look sharp on the patio of this modern A-frame in the mountains.

# SWING +

Hanging a swing in your home or yard is the perfect way to satisfy and nurture your inner child. How can anyone be in a grumpy mood after swinging, even for just a few minutes?

Though the pattern calls for a wooden board from which to make the seat, your swing doesn't need to be a perfect rectangle, or even made of wood. Substitute whatever you'd like for the wooden board as long as its size is similar to the one given—and, even more important, as long as it is strong enough to safely hold the weight of an adult in motion! For example, on a beach walk years ago, I found a large piece of driftwood, lugged it up the hill, and saved it for a project someday. When the idea for this swing came to be, the driftwood, with just a little sanding, made a perfect seat. (See photo, page 143.) You might also try using paint or playing with color—if ever there was a project that called for some extra whimsy, this is it.

**FINISHED SIZE**
8'6" long, from top of ring to bottom of fringe, by 20" wide

**KNOTS & TECHNIQUES**
Lark's Head Knot (LHK), page 23

Half Square Knot (HSK), page 24

Square Knot (SK), page 25

Sinnet of Square Knots, page 27

Half Square Knot Spiral, page 27

Bundling, page 33

**SUGGESTED SETUP**
C-Clamp, page 18

**SUPPLIES**
280' white cotton rope (5mm diameter)

20" length of 2" by 8" wooden board

Two 3–5" brass rings

Swivel clip

4 rubber bands

Drill and ½" drill bit

Painter's or masking tape

**CUT LIST**
Four 50' lengths

Four 20' lengths

CONTINUED

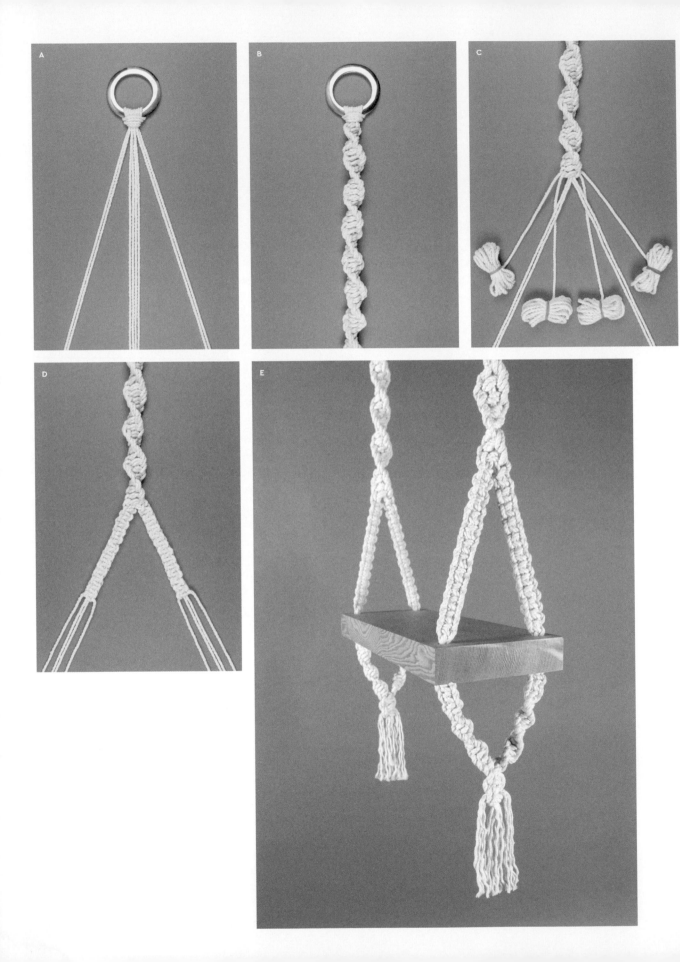

## PREPARATION

**1** Drill a ½"-diameter hole 1" from each corner of the board. Before making the holes, it may be helpful to place a piece of tape on the underside of the board beneath the points at which you plan to drill. This helps minimize tearing and splitting of the wood around the holes. Remove the tape after drilling.

**2** Because the cords will be held double throughout the first portion of this project, it's helpful to pair off the ropes before you begin knotting. Start by taping two of the 50' ropes together at the center; then bundle together the 2 cords, on either side of the tape, with rubber bands. Repeat with the remaining two 50' lengths; then tape the 2 pairs of 20' ropes together at the center without bundling.

**3** Hang the swivel clip from a secured C-clamp and clip it onto one of the brass rings.

## KNOTTING

**4** Pick up 1 pair of ropes of each length. Mount all 4 ropes together onto the prepared ring using an LHK, making sure that the center of each rope is at the center of the knot. Then bring the shorter cords to the center of the group and remove the tape. [A]

**5** Using the bundled cords as working cords and the shorter cords as filler cords, work a 7'-long HSK spiral with the cords held double. Space your HSKs so that you have about 24 HSKs per 1' of knotting. [B]

**6** Remove the rubber bands from the pairs of working cords and rebundle the cords individually. Bring 1 working cord to either side of each pair of filler cords. [C]

**7** Work two 8" sinnets of SKs. [D]

**8** Tape the ends of each group of 4 cords together, and thread them through the holes on one of the short sides of the board.

**9** With each group of 4 cords, work a column consisting of 2 SKs followed by a 4" HSK spiral.

**10** Bring all 8 cords together and work 2 SKs with the cords held double.

**11** Repeat steps 3–10 to complete the other side of the swing.

## FINISHING

**12** Trim the cords to 7" and unravel them. [E]

### NOTES

This swing is designed to be hung at a height of 10'. For lower ceilings, adjust the length of the spiral accordingly.

To avoid running out of rope before you are finished, be sure to maintain even knot spacing as you work. Take a minute to measure and count your knots periodically, and adjust them as needed.

# SUMMER SLING CHAIR ++

When I came across this chair base, I knew it needed to be updated with macramé. With the addition of simple stripes making it fresh and modern, this sling chair is great for a patio, by the pool, or in a sunroom. Relax into it with a book and your favorite summer beverage, or toss a pair in your car for a stylish addition to your camping setup.

Since these chairs are knotted with cotton, I recommend bringing them indoors when the weather isn't great. They fold up nicely and store flat, so it's easy to move them. They will last much longer this way, so you can enjoy your handiwork for years to come!

**FINISHED SIZE**
43" length, laid flat, by 18" seat width

**KNOTS & TECHNIQUES**
Square Knot (SK), page 25

Right-Facing Square Knot (RSK), page 25

Sinnet of Square Knots, page 27

Sinnet of Right-Facing Square Knots, page 27

Alternating Rows of Square Knots, page 29

Alternating Rows/Rounds of Two (or More) Square Knots, page 29

Bundling, page 33

**SUPPLIES**
Main Color Rope (MC): 360' white cotton rope (5mm diameter)

Contrast Color Rope (CC): 420' light gray cotton rope (5mm diameter)

Sling chair frame that can accommodate 18" of seat width

26 rubber bands

Washi or masking tape

12mm plastic or metal crochet hook

**CUT LIST**
Twelve 30' lengths MC

Fourteen 30' lengths CC

CONTINUED

## PREPARATION

**1** Bundle all of the ropes with rubber bands and tape the ends to prevent unraveling.

**2** Fold 1 MC rope in half and feed its looped end from top to bottom through the slit at the front of the chair frame until the loop hangs down a few inches below. Repeat with the remaining ropes, arranging them in the following order: 2 MC, 4 CC, 4 MC, 6 CC, 4 MC, 4 CC, 2 MC. It may be helpful to use a thin crochet hook or other small object with a dull point to push the loops through the slit.

**3** Thread one of the dowels that came with your chair frame through the loops, making sure the cords stay in order and don't become twisted around one another. [A]

**4** Sit facing the front of the chair frame, and bring the cords toward you over the slit, again being careful to keep them in order. To avoid having the chair frame in your way while you work, you will be knotting the seat with its underside facing up. Because SKs and RSKs are reversible, you can choose to work on any project made from these knots in this way.

## SEAT

The seat is made of netting consisting of alternating rows of 2-knot sinnets of left-facing square knots (SKs) and right-facing square knots (RSKs). The two knot types are arranged strategically within each row to create symmetrical stripes down the seat.

**5** Work the following rows from left to right, tightening the knots in the first row thoroughly so that the dowel is held securely in place.

Row 1: Work 6 sinnets of 2 RSKs and then 7 sinnets of 2 SKs.

Row 2: Skip the first 2 cords and then work 1 sinnet of 2 RSKs, 3 sinnets of 2 SKs, 2 sinnets of 2 RSKs, 2 sinnets of 2 SKs, 3 sinnets of 2 RSKs, and 1 sinnet of 2 SKs. Skip the last 2 cords. [B]

**6** Repeat Rows 1–2 until the knotting measures about 43" in length, ending with a Row 1.

CONTINUED

## BACK

7 Flip the knotting over onto the chair frame and thread each cord through the slit at the top. Pull the cords down until the knotting rests against the frame on the front side of the slit. [C]

8 Weave the remaining dowel through the cords. Then, work the following rows from left to right.

Row 1: 7 SKs and 6 RSKs while tightening each knot thoroughly to secure the dowel in place. As you work this row, make sure that the top of the knotting of the seat sits flush against the front side of the slit. Pull the working cords taut before working each knot. Once the row is finished, take a moment to pull the filler cords of each knot down as well.

Row 2: Skip the first 2 cords and then work 1 sinnet of 2 SKs, 3 sinnets of 2 RSKs, 2 sinnets of 2 SKs, 2 sinnets of 2 RSKs, 3 sinnets of 2 SKs, and 1 sinnet of 2 RSKs. Skip the last 2 cords.

Row 3: Work 7 sinnets of 2 SKs and then 6 sinnets of 2 RSKs. [D]

Row 4: Skip 6 cords, work 1 sinnet of 2 RSKs, skip 4 cords, work 1 sinnet of 2 RSKs, skip 4 cords, work 1 sinnet of 2 SKs, work 1 sinnet of 2 RSKs, skip 4 cords, work 1 sinnet of 2 SKs, skip 4 cords, work 1 sinnet of 2 SKs, and then skip 6 cords.

Row 5: Work a sinnet of 2 SKs using the 4 centermost cords. [E]

9 Bring the cords together into 7 tassels from left to right as follows.

1st tassel: Work a sinnet of 2 SKs 2" below using the leftmost 4 cords.

2nd and 3rd tassels: With the next 8 cords, work a sinnet of 2 RSKs using the first and eighth cords as working cords and the cords between them as filler. Repeat with the next 8 cords.

4th (center) tassel: With the next 12 cords, work a sinnet of 2 SKs using the first and twelfth cords as working cords and the cords between them as filler cords.

5th and 6th tassels: With the next 8 cords, work a sinnet of 2 SKs using the first and eighth cords as working cords, and the cords between them as filler cords. Repeat with the next 8 cords.

7th tassel: Work a sinnet of 2 RSKs 2" below using the last 4 cords. [F]

## FINISHING

10 Trim the cords extending from all but the 4th (center) tassel 6" below the knotting.

11 Trim the 4th tassel in line with the others, and unravel all of the cords. [G]

# HOOP CHAIR ++

A classic shape, the hoop chair has been a style staple since the 1950s and has, like macramé, made a resurgence. When I was in Haiti in 2014, a metalsmith lived across the street from the artisan workshop where I taught. I saw him sitting in a small version of the hoop chair and asked if he would make me one to macramé on. By the end of the week, I had it in my hands and spent my final afternoon in the workshop sitting cross-legged on the tile floor, knotting simple square knots on the frame. The result was a clean and modern twist on a classic.

**FINISHED SIZE**

Overall Dimensions: 30" hoop diameter by 25" tall

Seat Dimensions: 19" tall by 21" wide by 18" deep

**KNOTS & TECHNIQUES**

Reverse Lark's Head Knot (RLHK), page 23

Square Knot (SK), page 25

Right-Facing Square Knot (RSK), page 25

Sinnet of Square Knots, page 27

Alternating Square Knots (ASK), page 28

Alternating Rows of Square Knots, page 29

Bundling, page 33

**SUPPLIES**

696' white cotton rope (5mm diameter)

Hoop chair frame

8 rubber bands

Washi or masking tape

**CUT LIST**

Four 20' lengths

Forty-four 14' lengths

CONTINUED

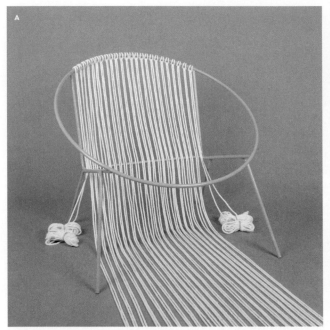

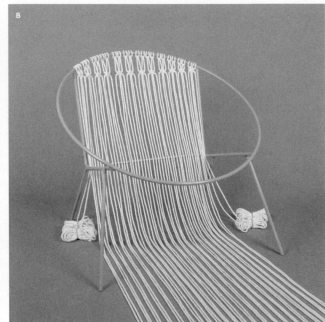

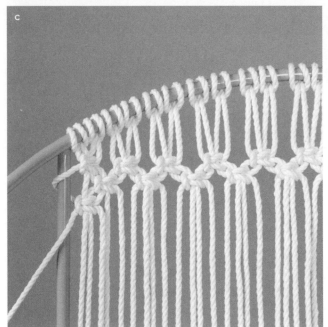

• Work your knots tightly throughout this project. This helps prevent the seat from sagging excessively with use.

## PREPARATION

1 Tape the ends of all the ropes and bundle the 20' lengths with rubber bands.

## BACK

2 Mount 22 of the 14' ropes onto the hoop frame between the vertical bars using RLHKs; then mount one 20' bundled rope at either end. Space them evenly. [A]

Row 1: Work a row of SKs, keeping the knots level rather than hugging the curved edge of the frame. If you'd like, mark this height with a piece of tape before knotting to help keep this row of knots level. [B]

Row 2: Work a row of ASKs.

Row 3: Wrap the leftmost cord in front of and then around the vertical bar to its left, and pull it taut. [C] Then, work ASKs until you reach the last 4 cords. Wrap the rightmost cord in front of and then around the vertical bar to its right, pull it taut, and work an SK with the last 4 cords.

Rows 4–24: Repeat Rows 2–3 until you have worked a total of 24 rows, or until the bottom of the knots in the last row reaches the bar at the back of the seat when stretched taut, ending with a Row 2.

## SEAT

3 Tip the frame so that the back rests on the floor and the seat is facing you. Then, mount all of the remaining ropes onto the hoop between the vertical bars, exactly as you did for the back. Be sure to include the remaining two 20' ropes, placing one at either end as you did for the back.

Row 1: Work a row of RSKs, keeping the knots level rather than hugging the curved edge of the frame.

Row 2: Work an alternating row of RSKs.

Row 3: Wrap the leftmost cord behind and then around the bar to its left, pull it taut, and then work alternating RSKs until you reach the last 4 cords. Wrap the rightmost cord behind and then around the bar to its right, pull it taut, and then work an RSK with the last 4 cords.

Rows 4–21: Repeat Rows 2–3 until you have worked a total of 21 rows, or until the bottom of the knots in the last row reaches the bar at the back of the seat when stretched taut, ending with a Row 3. [D]

CONTINUED

## JOINING THE BACK TO THE SEAT

**4** Set the chair upright with the back facing you, and organize the cords as follows.

i. Push all the cords away from you to the other side of the bar at the back of the seat.

ii. Pull each pair of the seat's filler cords toward you, bringing them over the bar so that they divide the cords of the back into groups of four.

iii. Next, you will bring groups of 4 seat cords between the groups of 4 back cords. To do this, bring the working cords of each SK in the last row of the seat toward you, between the groups of 4 cords of the back and beneath the bar at the back of the seat, and combine them with their filler cords. [E]

**5** Work a row of SKs, using the groups of 4 seat cords; then pull each set of filler cords down and toward you to thoroughly tighten the knots. [F]

**6** Tip the chair onto its back with the bottom of the seat facing you, and use the cords extending from the back of the chair to work a row of SKs securely tightened beneath the seat.

## FINISHING

**7** Set the chair upright again with the back facing you. Bring all of the cords toward you. Pick up the leftmost 16 cords (i.e., the cords extending from the leftmost 2 SKs in both of the last two rows). Use the first and eighth cords in the row closest to you to work a sinnet of 3 SKs around the remaining 14 cords. Repeat with the remaining cords.

**8** Trim all cords 6" below the knotting. [G]

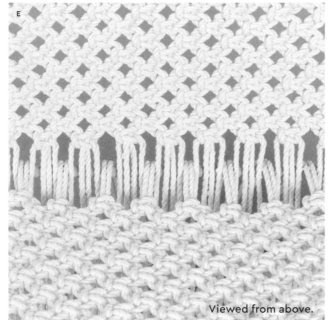

Viewed from above.

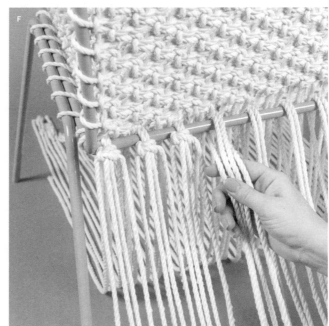

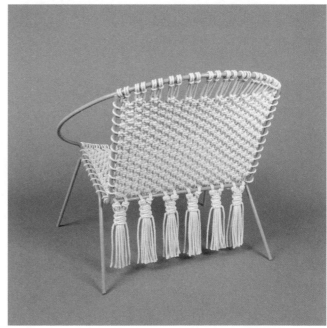

# DAYBED ++

I'm obsessed with thrift-store shopping and going to estate sales. You never know what kind of treasures you might find. Most discoveries are in pristine shape, but some things that I have collected over the years have needed fixing. Recently, my sweetheart placed a moratorium on bringing anything home that needed repairs, for both our sakes. We are optimists at heart, but the piles of objects that needed fixing were growing.

This daybed project came from one of those "needing love" objects. I found a cool vintage army cot at a yard sale; the canvas was rotting away and had a few tears, but my plan was to get nice new canvas and re-cover the wooden frame.

I pulled off the old fabric and decided instead to use the frame to macramé on! A unique piece of furniture was born. Since then, I've found a great supplier of new cots (see Resources, page 240) that are sturdier (and sans mold) on which to make macramé, but I am still grateful for that original yard-sale find.

**FINISHED SIZE**
84½" long by 37½" wide by 18" tall

**KNOTS & TECHNIQUES**
Reverse Lark's Head Knot (RLHK), page 23

Square Knot (SK), page 25
Sinnet of Square Knots, page 27
Alternating Square Knots (ASK), page 28

**SUPPLIES**
1,036' white cotton rope (5mm diameter)
Cot frame

**CUT LIST**
Two 25' lengths
Fifty-eight 17' lengths

CONTINUED

- In this pattern, the "sides" of the frame are the long sides of the rectangle.
- Work your knots tightly throughout this project. This helps prevent the cot from sagging excessively with use.

## PREPARATION

1  Assemble the cot frame per manufacturer's instructions.

2  Mount all of the 17' ropes onto one side of the frame using RLHKs. Make sure that half of the ropes are mounted to the left of the center leg and half to the right, and that the farthest rope on either side is mounted on the outside of the leg next to it. This enables you to anchor the corners of your knotting around the legs at the head and foot of the frame.

## KNOTTING

3  Work a row of SKs. If you have mounted your ropes correctly, you will have worked an SK directly above each of the three legs. [A]

4  Work 16 rows of ASKs, 1¼" apart, or until your knotting can just barely be stretched to reach the other side of the frame, ending with a row that has SKs at both ends.

5  To prepare the cords for knotting around the opposite side of the frame, first bring the leftmost cord to the left of the leg next to it and underneath the corner of the frame. Then bring the cord on its right over the side of the frame. Repeat with the 2 cords on the far right. Position all of the remaining filler cords from the previous row under the frame and the working cords over it.

6  Skipping the outermost 2 cords on either end, work a row of SKs beneath the frame. You should still have about 1¼" of rope

between the knots in this row and those in the previous one. [B]

7  Pull each pair of filler cords down and toward yourself until the last SK rests below the edge of the frame. [C]

8  Mount one of the 25' ropes onto the far right end of the side of the frame. [D] Wrap both of its cords around the bar at the end of the frame and between the rows of ASKs, stretching the knotting taut. [E]

9  When you reach the opposite corner, bring 1 cord up through the frame and the other underneath, and bring them together again at the outside edge of the frame. Combine both cords with the 2 cords to their left. Then pull all 4 cords taut and use them to work an SK in line with the others at the edge of the frame. [F]

10  Repeat steps 8–9 on the left.

11  Work 2 rows of ASKs, ½" apart.

12  The next row is a row of 2 SK sinnets with the cords held double, worked 1" below the previous one; however, it needs to be offset by 2 cords to achieve the desired look. To do this, work the leftmost sinnet of 2 SKs with 6 filler cords and the rightmost sinnet with only 2 filler cords. Work all other sinnets with 4 filler cords. Work all with the working cords held double.

13  With the exception of the outermost sinnets of the previous row, use the centermost 4 cords of each group to work an SK 1" below.

## FINISHING

14  Trim the cords of each tassel in a V-shape that extends 5½" below the knotting at its lowest point, and unravel them. [G]

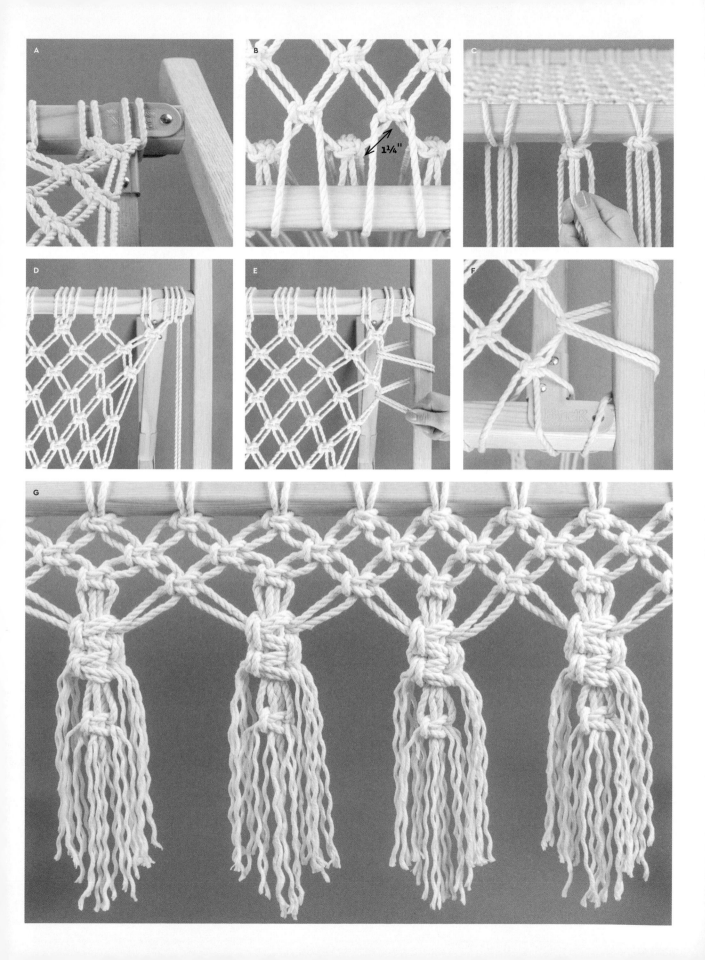

# RUGS

The floor might not be the first place we think of putting macramé but it can be an inspired choice. Not only is knotwork beautiful and durable underfoot, each step on it is like a tiny foot massage! My obsession with rugs (and foot massages) brought the two very different patterns in this chapter into being, one thick and dense with luxurious fiber, and the other small, simple, and clean.

Made in classic jute, the Welcome Home Accent Rug does its humble job well, serving as a doormat or a patch of geometric intrigue on a light-colored floor. One great virtue of a simple pattern is that it can easily be altered in size and/or material, and the texture of the simple knotting underfoot varies immensely depending on the material with which it is worked. The same rug in wool would have an entirely different feel. And one made in cotton might make for a sweet, nubby bath mat.

The second pattern in this chapter has entirely different strengths. The Many Diamonds Rug is made of fantastically giant, hand-felted yarn from Nepal. Both the yarn's rich texture and the rug's diamond pattern radiate warmth and a feeling both homey and a bit decadent. Beside your bed as the first thing beneath your feet in the morning or cozied in your favorite reading nook, this rug is sure to inspire long conversations. Your knotwork will be the center of attention.

Above: The Many Diamonds Rug (page 178) is stunning in whatever colorways you choose. On the left, charcoal, yellow, cream, and brown look modern and chic in an intimate library. On the right, cream, charcoal, and brown are gorgeous beneath an illuminated staircase.

Opposite: This bath mat, a variant use of the Welcome Home Accent Rug (page 173), would be a lovely addition to a relaxing afternoon spent soaking in a tub.

# WELCOME HOME ACCENT RUG ++

I'm an avid collector of textiles, with piles of rugs around the house, but finding the right doormat has proven a challenge. Of course, this is exactly why it pays to be a maker—when you can't find something you want, you can make it yourself! So I knotted up just the thing I wanted, a functional, everyday basic that is adaptable in style and purpose depending on the materials used. On the following pages, you'll find its basic pattern, plus a few variations to use as a springboard for making just the thing you want for *your* space.

**FINISHED SIZE**
22" wide by 28" long, plus 7" fringe at each end

**KNOTS & TECHNIQUES**
Lark's Head Knot (LHK), page 23

Square Knot (SK), page 25

Alternating Rows/Rounds of Two (or More) Square Knots, page 29

Horizontal Double Half Hitch (HDHH), page 30

**SUGGESTED SETUP**
Supported Dowel or Hanging Dowel, page 18

**SUPPLIES**
514' jute rope (¼" diameter)

Washi or masking tape

**CUT LIST**
Twenty-eight 18' lengths

Two 5' lengths

CONTINUED

## PREPARATION

1 Tape off a 22" workspace on the dowel.

2 Mount all twenty-eight 18' ropes on the dowel using LHKs and space them evenly across the workspace.

3 Starting from the center of an LHK, measure 7" around the dowel and down the front of the leftmost cord. Mark this point with a piece of tape. Repeat on the right; then connect the two points by gently securing a length of tape horizontally across all of the cords, making sure they remain evenly spaced and are not twisted. [A]

## KNOTTING

• Be sure to tighten each HDHH just enough to keep it positioned directly below the LHK above it. If your knots aren't tight enough, then this row will end up wider than you'd like. If they are too tight, the row will be too narrow.

• Be careful not to incorporate the ends of the filler cord into the subsequent knotting.

4 Leaving an 8" tail, work a row of HDHHs from left to right around one of the 5' ropes using the tape line as a guide and removing it as you work your way across. [B]

5 Work 19 alternating rows of 2 SKs, or until you have roughly 12" of rope remaining on each cord. Be sure to end with a row that has SKs at its left and right edges. [C]

6 Directly below the last row of 2 SKs, work a row of HDHHs from left to right using the other 5' rope as the filler cord, and again leaving an approximately 8"-long tail in the filler cord before knotting.

## FINISHING

7 Trim all of the cords along the bottom edge, as well as both ends of the filler cords from the 2 rows of HDHH, to about 7". [D]

8 To create fringe at the top, cut each rope at the center of its LHK. [E] Snip one near the middle first; then work your way out toward the edges. [F]

## VARIATIONS

TRY A DIFFERENT TYPE OF ROPE: The simple design of this rug lends itself to a variety of materials, from cotton to wool to synthetics. If you choose a rope with a different diameter than the one given, be aware that the size of your finished rug will differ, as will the amount of material you will need to complete it. Be sure to begin by working up a swatch (see page 34) of the knotting pattern in your chosen material.

MAKE STRIPES: Use multiple colors of rope to create vertical striping. Choose an allover striping pattern for a more traditional look or experiment with asymmetry!

TRY A DIFFERENT KNOTTING PATTERN: The allover knotting pattern I used is just one option of many that would work here. Simple ASKs would work beautifully as well, or try your hand at designing your own repeating SK pattern. As long as the knot spacing is similar to that in the pattern, you can simply use the given cut list unchanged. I don't recommend using a less-dense knotting pattern than the one given, as it may result in a rug that is fragile and lumpy underfoot.

SHORTEN THE FRINGE: The fringe can be trimmed as short as 4" without sacrificing durability.

CONTINUED

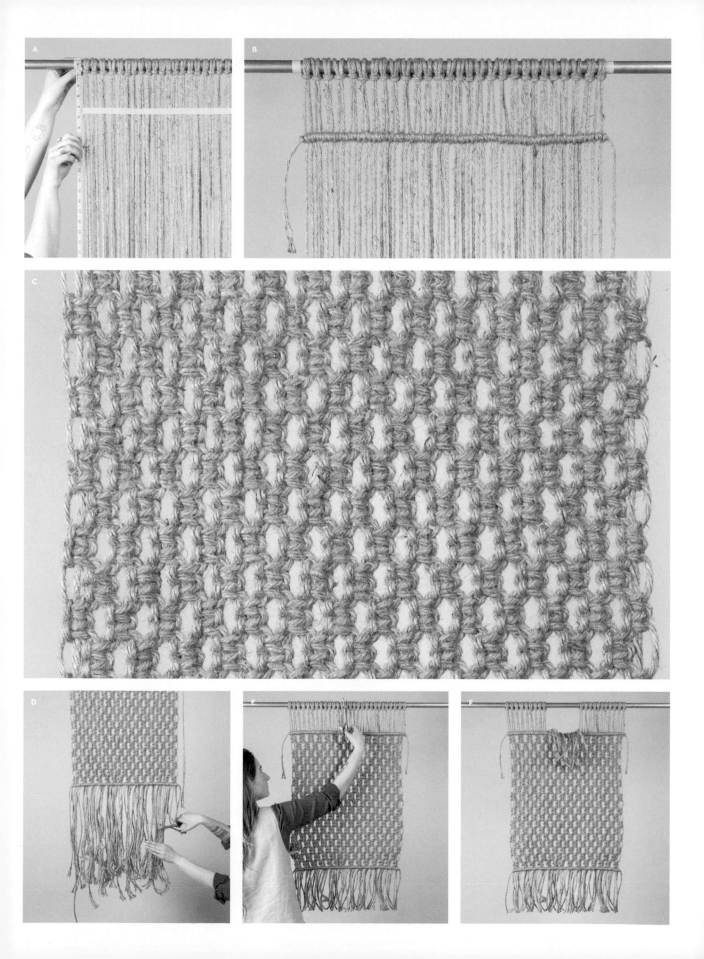

ADJUST THE WIDTH: To make a rug of a different width, you will need to adjust two things, the number of ropes used for knotting and the length of the two shorter ropes used as filler cords for the HDHHs.

A.   How many knotting ropes? You will need to cut about 1.25 knotting ropes per 1 inch of desired width. To determine the number of ropes you will need for a rug of any width, multiply your desired width (in inches) by 1.25 and then round your answer down to the nearest even number. This is the number of knotting ropes you need to cut. For example, for a rug that is 36" wide:

$36 \times 1.25 = 45$

So, 45 rounded down to the nearest even number gives you 44 ropes in all. Once you've determined how many ropes you will need, tape off a workspace of your desired width and space this number of ropes evenly across it. If you'd like to change the length of your rug as well, see Adjust the Length (at right) before you start cutting.

B.   How long should the filler cords be? These ropes need to be as long as your piece is wide, plus 14" for fringe and about 4" for wiggle room. To make a 36"-wide rug, for example, you would need two ropes of 54" each, one for each row of HDHH.

ADJUST THE LENGTH: To change the length of the rug, you will need to adjust the length of the knotting ropes. For each 1 inch of finished rug length, you will need about 7¼ inches of rope length. To calculate the total length needed for each knotting rope, multiply your desired rug length (excluding fringe) by 7.25, then add 14" for fringe. For example, for a rug that is 60" long:

$60 \times 7.25 = 435"$

$435 + 14 = 449"$ (37'5") of length per rope

# MANY DIAMONDS RUG +++

Patterned rugs, as they say, really tie a room together. And with this project, you get to tie the knots that tie a room together! Dad jokes aside, this project is a bit of a challenge. It requires the most skill and patience of any in this book. To make it, you will need to solve its puzzle and find your inner sculptor, subtly manipulating the knots into shape as you work. Pay attention, read the instructions carefully, take deep breaths, and enjoy making the pattern take shape.

At home, rugs aren't only for the floors. You can hang them on the wall, too. Just because this project was designed as a rug, don't feel like you can't throw it over the back of a sofa or hang it over your bed to add texture and softness and maybe a pop of color.

**FINISHED SIZE**
3' wide by 4'3" long, plus fringe

**KNOTS & TECHNIQUES**
Lark's Head Knot (LHK), page 33

Horizontal Double Half Hitch Knot (HDHH), page 30

Mounting with an HDHH, page 31

Horizontal Triple Half Hitch Knot (HTHH), page 32

Bundling, page 33

**SUGGESTED SETUP**
Hanging Dowel, page 18

**SUPPLIES**
Main Color Yarn (MC): Nine 50-yd balls Love Fest Fibers "Tough Love" felt yarn in Natural

Contrast Color Yarn (CC): One 50-yd ball Love Fest Fibers "Tough Love" felt yarn in Cocoa

Contrast Color Two Yarn (CC2): One 50-yd ball Love Fest Fibers "Tough Love" felt yarn in Charcoal Gray

50 rubber bands

Washi or masking tape

**CUT LIST**
Eight 60' lengths in MC*

Thirteen 50' lengths in MC*

Two 50' lengths in CC

Four 6' lengths in CC

Two 30' lengths in CC2

Two 6' lengths in CC2

One 2' length in CC2

* After cutting your MC yarn, you will have several long pieces left over. Ball or bundle them up so they don't get tangled, and keep them to use as filler cord throughout the rug. If you run out of filler cord before your rug is finished, see Joining New Yarn to a Filler Cord, page 157, for instructions on how to add in a new length of filler cord.

CONTINUED

Finished rug, front.

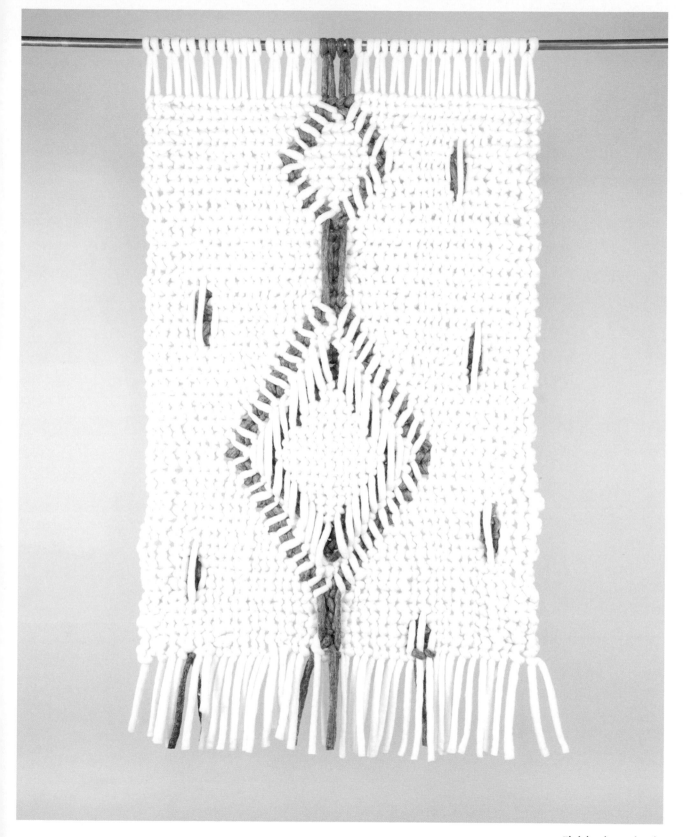

Finished rug, back.

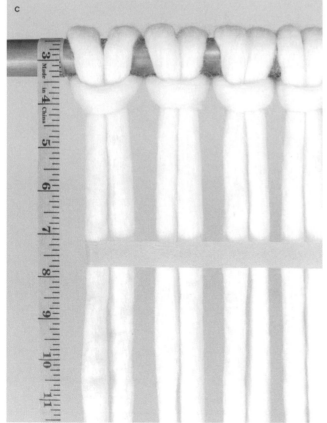

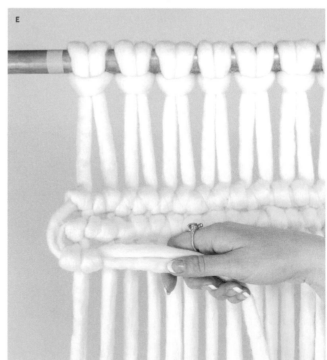

## PREPARATION

**1** Bundle each 60', 50', and 30' rope with rubber bands, keeping them carefully organized by length.

**2** Tape off a 3' workspace on the dowel.

**3** Using LHKs, mount ropes in the following order from left to right: two 60' in MC, three 50' in MC, one 60' in MC, four 50' in MC, one 60' in MC, two 50' in CC, one 60' in MC, four 50' in MC, one 60' in MC, two 50' in MC, and two 60' in MC. Space them evenly across your workspace. [A]

**4** Tape the ends of the four mounted CC cords and label them from left to right with the numbers 1–4. From left to right, label the 5 MC cords on left of the CC cords H, I, J, K, L. Label the 5 MC cords on the right of the CC cords M, N, O, P, Q. [B]

**5** Starting from the center of the leftmost LHK, measure 7" around the dowel and down the front of the leftmost cord. Mark this height with a piece of tape. Repeat on the right, and then connect the two points by gently securing a length of tape horizontally across all of the cords, making sure they remain evenly spaced and are not twisted. [C]

## KNOTTING

• Except where otherwise specified, all knots in this pattern are HDHHs.

• Keeping the knotting and overall shape of the rug looking neat can be tricky. Be sure to tighten your knots firmly and evenly, and that each finished row measures 3' in width.

**6** Work odd-numbered rows from left to right and even-numbered rows from right to left.

Row 1: Pick up the longest piece of excess MC yarn to use as a filler cord. Leaving an 8" tail in the filler cord, work HDHHs around it until you reach the labeled cords, work Row 1 of Diamond (see chart on page 188), and then work HDHHs to the end. Measure to make sure the row is 3' wide, and adjust your knotting if necessary. Repeat this process of measuring and adjusting at the end of every row to keep the width of your rug even. [D]

Row 2: Work HDHHs until you reach the labeled cords, work Row 2 of Diamond, and then work to the end.

Row 3: Work the first several HDHHs of this row around both the tail from the beginning of Row 1 and the filler cord [E], and then trim the tail as close to the knotting as possible. This helps keep the edge of the first row of knotting from unraveling over time. Work until you reach the labeled cords, work Row 3 of Diamond, and then work to the end.

Row 4: Work to the labeled cords, work Row 4 of Diamond, and then work to the end.

Row 5: Work 7 HDHHS. Label the next 3 cords A, B, and C, and then work the first row of Tiny Diamond A (see page 186), using a 6' length in CC. Work to the next group of labeled cords, work Row 5 of Diamond, and then work to the end.

Row 6: Work to the labeled cords, work Row 6 of Diamond, work to the next labeled cords, work Row 2 of Tiny Diamond A, and then work to the end.

Row 7: Work to the labeled cords, work Row 3 of Tiny Diamond A, work to the next labeled cords, work Row 7 of Diamond, and then work to the end.

Row 8: Work to the labeled cords, work Row 8 of Diamond, work to the next labeled cords, work Row 4 of Tiny Diamond A, and then work to the end.

CONTINUED

Row 9: Work to the labeled cords, work Row 5 of Tiny Diamond A, work to the next labeled cords, work Row 9 of Diamond, and then work to the end.

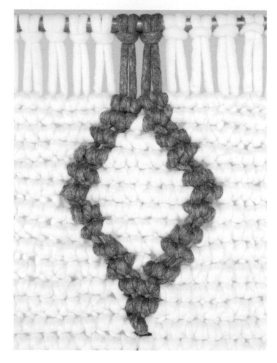

Row 10: Work to the labeled cords, work Row 10 of Diamond, work to the next labeled cords, work Row 6 of Tiny Diamond A, and then work to the end.

Row 11: Work to the labeled cords, work Row 11 of Diamond, and then work to the end.

Row 12: Work to the labeled cords, work Row 12 of Diamond, and then work to the end.

Row 13: Work to the labeled cords, work Row 13 of Diamond, and then work to the end.

Row 14: Work the first 10 MC cords. Tape the ends of the next 7 cords, and label them from left to right with the letters A–G. Work cords A–L, skip all CC cords, and then work cords M–Q.

Tape the next 7 cords and label them from left to right with the letters R–X. Work cords R–X, and then continue to the end.

Row 15: Work to the labeled cords, work Row 1 of Double Diamond (see chart on page 189), and then work to the end.

Row 16: Work 5 HDHHs, and then label the next 3 cords from left to right with the letters A, B, and C. Work Row 1 of Tiny Diamond B (see page 187), using a 6' length in CC. Work Row 2 of Double Diamond, and then work to the end.

Row 17: Work to the labeled cords, work Row 3 of Double Diamond, work Row 2 of Tiny Diamond B, and then work to the end.

Row 18: Work to the labeled cords, work Row 3 of Tiny Diamond B, work Row 4 of Double Diamond, and then work to the end.

Row 19: Work 5 HDHHs, and then label the next 3 cords A, B, and C. Work Row 1 of Tiny Diamond A across the cords you just labeled, using a 6' length of CC2. Work to the next labeled cords, work Row 5 of Double Diamond, work Row 4 of Tiny Diamond B, and then work to the end.

Row 20: Work to the labeled cords, work Row 5 of Tiny Diamond B, work Row 6 of Double Diamond, mounting a 30' length of CC2 onto the filler cord using an HDHH when you get to the "+" sign and then labeling its left and right cords 5 and 8, respectively. Work to the next labeled cords, work Row 2 of Tiny Diamond A, and then work to the end.

Row 21: Work to the labeled cords, work Row 3 of Tiny Diamond A, work to the next labeled cords, work Row 7 of Double Diamond, work Row 6 of Tiny Diamond B, and then work to the end.

Row 22: Work to the labeled cords, work Row 8 of Double Diamond, mounting a 30' length of CC2 onto the filler cord using an HDHH when you get to the "+" sign, and then labeling its left and right cords 6 and 7, respectively. Work to the next labeled cords, work Row 4 of Tiny Diamond A, and then work to the end.

Row 23: Work to the labeled cords, work Row 5 of Tiny Diamond A, work to the next labeled cords, work Row 9 of Double Diamond, and then work to the end.

Row 24: Work to the labeled cords, work Row 10 of Double Diamond, work to the labeled cords, work Row 6 of Tiny Diamond A, and then work to the end.

Row 25: Work to the labeled cords, work Row 11 of Double Diamond, and then work to the end.

Row 26: Work to the labeled cords, work Row 12 of Double Diamond, and then work to the end.

Row 27: Work to the labeled cords, work Row 13 of Double Diamond, and then work to the end.

Row 28: Work to the labeled cords, work Row 14 of Double Diamond, and then work to the end.

Row 29: Work to the labeled cords, work Row 15 of Double Diamond, and then work to the end.

Row 30: Work to the labeled cords, work Row 16 of Double Diamond, and then work to the end.

Row 31: Work to the labeled cords, work Row 17 of Double Diamond, and then work to the end.

Row 32: Work to the labeled cords, work Row 18 of Double Diamond, and then work to the end.

Row 33: Work 3 HDHHs and then label the next 3 cords from left to right A, B, and C. Work Row 1 of Tiny Diamond A across the cords you just labeled, using a 6' length of CC. Work to the next labeled cords, work Row 19 of Double Diamond, and then work to the end.

Row 34: Work to the labeled cords, work Row 20 of Double Diamond, work to the next labeled cords, work Row 2 of Tiny Diamond A, and then work to the end.

Row 35: Work to the labeled cords, work Row 3 of Tiny Diamond A, work to the next labeled cords, work Row 21 of Double Diamond, and then work to the end.

CONTINUED

Row 36: Work to the labeled cords, work Row 22 of Double Diamond, work to the next labeled cords, work Row 4 of Tiny Diamond A, and then work to the end.

Row 37: Work to the labeled cords, work Row 5 of Tiny Diamond A, work to the next labeled cords, work Row 23 of Double Diamond, work 1 HDHH, and then label the next 3 cords from left to right A, B, and C. Work Row 1 of Tiny Diamond A, using a 6' length in CC2. Work to the end.

Row 38: Work to the labeled cords, work Row 2 of Tiny Diamond A, work to the next labeled cords, work Row 24 of Double Diamond, work to the next labeled cords, work Row 6 of Tiny Diamond A, and then work to the end.

Row 39: Work to the labeled cords, work Row 25 of Double Diamond, work to the next labeled cords, work Row 3 of Tiny Diamond A, and then work to the end.

Row 40: Work to the labeled cords, work Row 4 of Tiny Diamond A, work to the next labeled cords, work Row 26 of Double Diamond, and then work to the end.

Row 41: Work to the labeled cords, work Row 27 of Double Diamond, work to the next labeled cords, work Row 5 of Tiny Diamond A, and then work to the end.

Row 42: Work to the labeled cords, work Row 6 of Tiny Diamond A, work to the next labeled cords, work Row 28 of Double Diamond, and then work to the end. Remove the labels from all MC cords except L, M, and N.

Row 43: Work 11 HDHHs, and then label the next 3 cords from left to right, A, B, and C. Work Row 1 of Tiny Diamond A, using a 6' length in CC. Work to the end, working HDHHs with all MC cords and skipping all CC cords.

Row 44: Work to the labeled cords. Work N, M, 2, L, and then K. Work to the labeled cords, work Row 2 of Tiny Diamond A, and then work to the end.

Row 45: Work to the labeled cords, work Row 3 of Tiny Diamond A, and then work to the next labeled cords. Work K, 2, 3, and then N. Work to the end.

Row 46: Work 5 HDHHs. Mount the 2' length of CC2 yarn onto the filler cord using an HDHH, and then work to the next labeled cords. Work 4, 3, M, 2, and then 1. Work to the next labeled cords, work Row 4 of Tiny Diamond A, and then work to the end.

## FINISHING

**7** Trim the cords at the bottom to 7" and remove any remaining tape.

**8** Remove the rug from the dowel by cutting each rope at the center of its LHK. Snip one near the middle first, and then work your way out toward the edges. (See Welcome Home Accent Rug, step 8, page 174.)

**9** Turn the rug over and tuck any loose ends into the knotting to conceal them.

## TINY DIAMOND A

Work odd rows from left to right, and even rows from right to left.

Row 1: Work A, skip B, mount a 6' length of CC (or CC2) yarn onto the filler cord using an HDHH, and then work C. Label the two new cords 1 and 2.

Row 2: Work 2, 1, and then A, skipping B and C.

Row 3: Skipping all 3 lettered cords, work an HTHH with 1 and then 2.

Row 4: Work C, 2, and then 1, skipping A and B.

Row 5: Work A, 1, and C, skipping B and 2.

Row 6: Work cords C, B, and A. Remove all labels.

## TINY DIAMOND B

Work odd rows from right to left, and even rows from left to right.

Row 1: Work C, skip B, mount a 6' length of CC (or CC2) yarn onto the filler cord using an HDHH, and then work A. Label the two new cords 1 and 2, from left to right.

Row 2: Work A, 1, and then 2, skipping B and C.

Row 3: Skip all 3 lettered cords, and work an HTHH with 2 and then 1.

Row 4: Work 1, 2, and then C, skipping A and B.

Row 5: Work C, 1, and then A, skipping B and 2.

Row 6: Work cords A, B, and C. Remove all labels.

### Joining New Yarn to a Working Cord

If one of your working cords comes up short, don't despair! Just spit-splice a new length of yarn onto the old one (see Felted, page 21) or follow these steps to add length.

1 Calculate how much more yarn is needed. You will need about 8" of yarn per row, plus 12". Cut a piece of yarn of this length.

2 Push the tail of the old working cord to the back and work an HDHH around the filler cord with the new working cord you just cut, leaving a 5" tail.

3 Push the tail of the new working cord to the back, and continue knotting.

### Joining New Yarn to A Filler Cord

If you run out of filler cord, you will need to add a new piece of yarn in order to continue. To do so, spit-splice another length onto the end of the old one (see Felted, page 21) or use the method here. Whenever possible, avoid joining yarn at the edge of the rug, as this may distort the rug's shape.

1 Work HDHHs until you're ready to join a new piece of yarn, making sure you have at least 4" of filler cord remaining.

2 Lay a new piece of MC yarn on top of the old one, pulling a tail of a few inches behind the last knot worked. [A]

3 Work HDHHs around both cords until the old filler cord runs out.

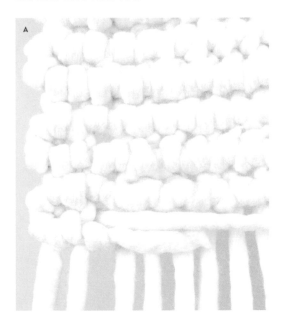

## DIAMOND

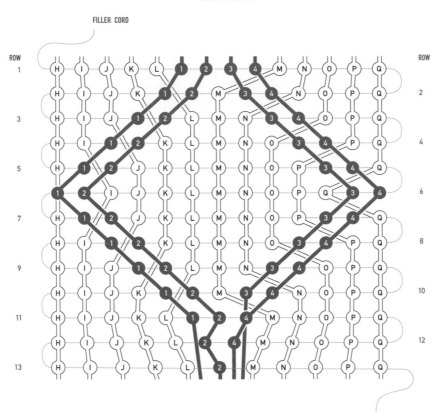

## HOW TO READ THE CHARTS IN THIS PATTERN

• Read and work all odd-numbered rows from left to right, and even-numbered rows from right to left.

• Each letter or number stands for 1 HDHH worked with the cord of that name.

• When you see a "+" sign, mount a new rope onto the filler cord using an HDHH.

• Always keep CC and CC2 cords in front of MC cords except in rows in which they are skipped.

• Be sure to note when cords are skipped, as they are in nearly every row. Also, be careful not to let the skipped cords become twisted around each other on the back side of the rug, as this may create lumps when the rug is placed on the floor. When in doubt, refer to the photograph on page 181 showing the completed back side of the rug.

# DOUBLE DIAMOND

# TABLETOP

An elevated tablescape is one in which every detail is considered, from the flatware to the candlesticks, dishware, glasses, and textiles. The four projects in this chapter offer a mix of stylish and utilitarian objects to enhance your dining experience, whether you are throwing a pizza party, an elaborate dinner, or simply making yourself a pot of tea.

From left: The Gathering Together Table Runner (page 199) and a bowl of citrus are a perfect balance to a gallery wall. The Kyoto Market Trivet (page 196) combines both beauty and function. The Ghost Ranch Place Mats (page 202) can be made in a variety of colors; here, contrasting cream and black set a refined table.

# KYOTO MARKET TRIVET +

Small, unassuming objects present opportunities for us to bring beauty into all aspects of our lives. An ordinary trivet is easy to find, but why not have a pretty handmade one instead? This little trivet was inspired by one I saw in a market in Kyoto and reminds me of the quiet power of details. Tuck it beneath your favorite tea kettle, hang it on a hook for pretty and easy storage, set a plant on it, or bring it to the table for a simple meal made special.

**FINISHED SIZE**
6½" diameter

**KNOTS & TECHNIQUES**
Square Knot (SK), page 25

Mounting with a Square Knot
(SK), see page 26

Overhand Knot (OK),
page 33

**SUPPLIES**
22' jute rope (¼" diameter)

6" metal hoop

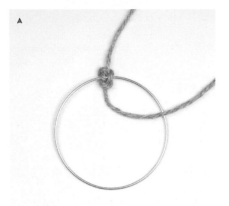

## KNOTTING

1  Mount the rope onto the hoop using an SK. [A]

2  Work SKs around the entire hoop. Press the knots close together as you work so that the hoop is completely concealed. [B]

## FINISHING

3  Make a 3" loop in one of the cords.

4  Wrap the other cord around the base of the loop twice. [C]

5  Tie both cords together tightly with 2 OKs, securing the loop in place. Trim the excess as close as possible to the OKs. [D]

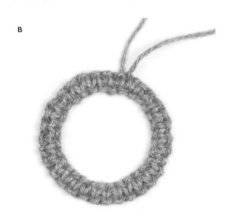

# GATHERING TOGETHER TABLE RUNNER +

There is nothing better than gathering together around a table with friends and delicious food and drink to share. This table runner was originally designed for a wedding photo shoot featuring macramé and florals at Union Pine, an event space in Portland. That table was aglow with crystals and candles. It also covered the table at the first ever Modern Macramé team holiday party, bringing a little bit of macramé magic to our celebration. Style this piece for a party or for every day. It looks great stretched out across a dining table but just as nice as a runner on a counter or coffee table.

**FINISHED SIZE**
10' long by 8" wide,
plus fringe

**KNOTS & TECHNIQUES**
Reverse Lark's Head Knot
(RLHK), page 23

Square Knot (SK), page 25

Alternating Square Knots
(ASK), page 28

Overhand Knot (OK),
page 33

**SUGGESTED SETUP**
Corkboard and Pins,
page 18

**SUPPLIES**
754' white cotton rope
(5mm diameter)

**CUT LIST**
One hundred twenty 6' lengths

Two 10' lengths

Eight 20" lengths (or longer,
if desired)

CONTINUED

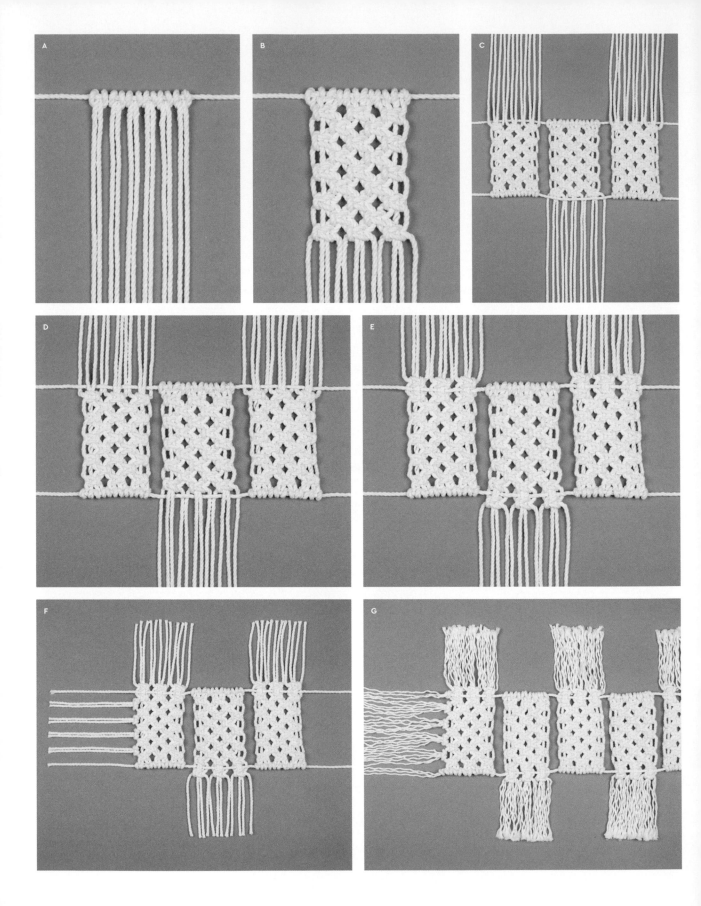

## PREPARATION

1 Place the corkboard on the floor or another stable, flat surface.

2 Pick up a 10' rope to use as a mounting cord and mount six of the 6' ropes onto it using RLHKs. Space the RLHKs evenly across 4" of the mounting cord. [A]

3 Use a few pins to secure the group of RLHKs to the corkboard. It is best to run the pins through the mounting cord, rather than the RLHKs themselves.

## KNOTTING

4 Work 9 rows of ASKs. [B]

5 Repeat steps 2–4 nine times on the same mounting cord. You should now have 10 identical panels.

6 Next, slide the panels into place along the mounting cord. First position the leftmost panel 10" from the left end of the mounting cord. Then space the remaining 9 panels out along the mounting cord, 6" apart. You should end up with about 16" of mounting cord remaining to the right of the last panel.

7 Repeat steps 2–6. You should now have two identical garlands.

8 Pin the first two panels of one garland onto the corkboard by again running the pins through the mounting cord at the top of each panel.

9 Rotate the second garland 180 degrees so that it faces the first. Center its first panel between those on the first garland, lining up the edge of each with the opposite garland's mounting cord. Make sure that the right sides of both garlands are facing up by checking that the RLHKs are facing up. You are now ready to join the garlands together. [C]

10 Organize the cords by bringing the pairs of filler cords in front of the mounting cords, and bringing the working cords behind them. [D]

11 Work a row of SKs across the end of each panel, securing the opposite garland's mounting cord inside the knots. [E]

## FINISHING

12 Cut the fringe on each panel to 5".

13 Add fringe to one end of the runner by using RLHKs to mount four 20" ropes along the outside edge of the last panel. [F]

14 Repeat step 13 at the opposite end of the runner.

15 Pick up one of the ends of either mounting cord. Use it to work an OK securely against the edge of the knotting. Repeat with the other 3 mounting cord ends.

16 Unravel all fringe. [G]

# GHOST RANCH PLACE MATS ++

Georgia O'Keeffe was enchanted by the land surrounding her ranch in Abiquiú, New Mexico, and it continues to inspire anyone who visits. Here, I incorporated a geometric design in a nod to my own Southwestern roots. A playful twist on a traditional macramé place mat, this pattern is for a set of two. I made mine in black, but you can choose any color to match your tablescape.

**FINISHED SIZE, EACH PIECE**
16½" wide by 17½" long, including fringe

**KNOTS & TECHNIQUES**
Lark's Head Knot (LHK), page 23

Square Knot (SK), page 25

Right-Facing Square Knot (RSK), page 25

Alternating Rows of Square Knots, page 29

Horizontal Double Half Hitch (HDHH), page 30

**SUGGESTED SETUP**
Supported Dowel or Hanging Dowel, page 18*

**SUPPLIES**
372' Hemptique hemp rope (4mm diameter)

Washi or masking tape

**CUT LIST**
Four 34" lengths

Thirty 12' lengths

*For this project it is important to use a dowel with a diameter of at least 1¼", as the size of the dowel determines the length of the fringe along the top edge.

CONTINUED

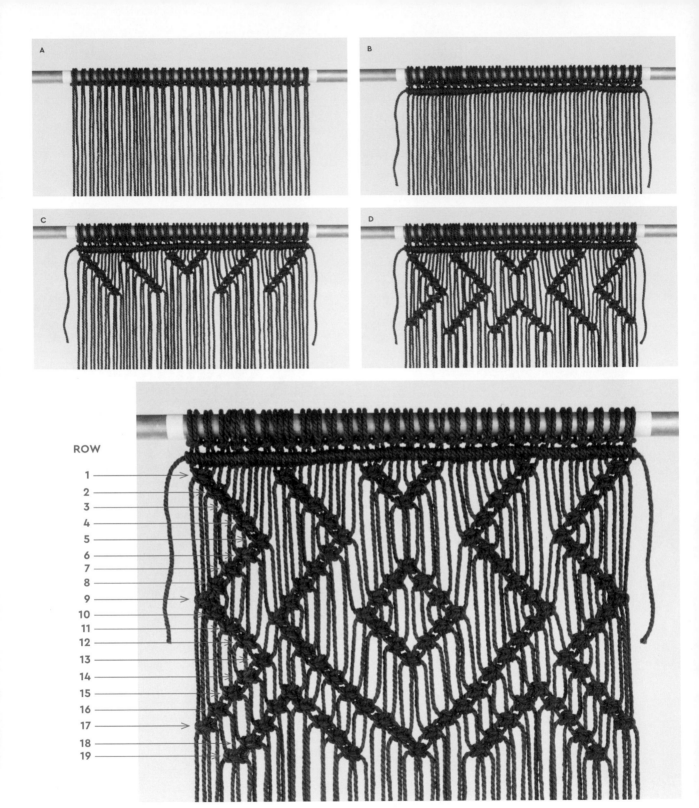

ROW

1
2
3
4
5
6
7
8
9
10
11
12
13
14
15
16
17
18
19

## PREPARATION

**1** Tape off a 16½" workspace on the dowel.

**2** Mount the thirty 12' ropes onto the dowel using LHKs, and space them evenly across your workspace. [A]

## KNOTTING

**3** Work a row of HDHHs from left to right, using a 34" rope as filler and leaving a tail of approximately 9" on either side of the knotting. Be sure to tighten each HDHH just enough to keep it positioned directly below the LHK above it. If your knots aren't tight enough, then this row will end up wider than the LHKs above it. If they are too tight, the row will be too narrow. [B]

**4** Because this design has bilateral symmetry, the method for working all rows will only be described from the left edge to the center. To work each row, simply complete the left side as written, work the central SK (where noted), and then follow the instructions for the left side once again in reverse using RSKs.

Row 1: Work an SK, skip 8 cords, work an SK, skip 8 cords, work an SK, skip 2 cords. Repeat in reverse.

Row 2: Skip 2 cords, work an SK, skip 8 cords, work an SK, skip 8 cords, work an SK. Repeat in reverse.

Row 3: Skip 4 cords, work an SK, skip 8 cords, work an SK, skip 8 cords. Work an SK in the center, and then repeat the left half of the row in reverse.

Row 4: Skip 6 cords, work an SK, skip 8 cords, work an SK, skip 8 cords. Repeat in reverse.

Row 5: Skip 8 cords, work an SK, skip 8 cords, work an SK, skip 6 cords. Repeat in reverse. [C]

Row 6: Repeat Row 4.

Row 7: Repeat Row 3.

Row 8: Repeat Row 2.

Row 9: Repeat Row 1. [D]

Row 10: Skip 2 cords, work an SK, skip 4 cords, work an SK, skip 8 cords, work an SK, skip 4 cords. Repeat in reverse.

Row 11: Skip 4 cords, work an SK, skip 4 cords, work an SK, skip 8 cords, work an SK, skip 2 cords. Repeat in reverse.

Row 12: Skip 6 cords, work an SK, skip 4 cords, work an SK, skip 8 cords, work an SK. Repeat in reverse.

Row 13: Skip 8 cords, work an SK, skip 4 cords, work an SK, skip 8 cords. Work an SK in the center and then repeat the left half of the row in reverse.

Row 14: Skip 6 cords, work an SK, skip 8 cords, work an SK, skip 8 cords. Repeat in reverse.

Row 15: Skip 4 cords, work an SK, skip 4 cords, work an SK, skip 4 cords, work an SK, skip 6 cords. Repeat in reverse.

Row 16: Skip 2 cords, work an SK, skip 4 cords, work 2 SKs, skip 4 cords, work an SK, skip 4 cords. Repeat in reverse.

Row 17: Work an SK, skip 4 cords, work an SK, skip 4 cords, work an SK, skip 4 cords, work an SK, skip 2 cords. Repeat in reverse.

Row 18: Skip 6 cords, work an SK, skip 8 cords, work an SK, skip 4 cords, work an SK. Repeat in reverse.

Row 19: Skip 4 cords, work an SK, skip 12 cords, work an SK, skip 4 cords. Work an SK in the center, and then repeat the left half of the row in reverse.

CONTINUED

5 Give the place mat a lower edge by working a row of HDHH from left to right, using a 34" rope as filler and leaving a tail of approximately 9" on either side of the knotting. [E]

6 Measure 7" below the previous row, and extend a piece of tape across all cords at this height. Work a row of HDHHs from left to right below the tape, using one of the 34" ropes as filler and leaving a tail of approximately 9" on either side of the knotting. [F]

7 Repeat steps 4–5 to make a second place mat below the first.

## FINISHING

8 Separate the place mats by carefully cutting the cords halfway between them. You may want to mark this height with a piece of tape before cutting to ensure that the fringe on each place mat is the same length. [G]

9 Trim all of the cords at the bottom to 3½" in length, including the tails extending from the lowest row of HDHHs.

10 Remove the first place mat from the dowel by cutting each rope at the center of its LHK. [H]

11 Trim the ropes you have just cut, as well as any remaining filler cords, to 3½" in length.

E

F

G

H

# WRAPPED VOTIVE +++

The shadows cast from these little votives make me so happy—I love the way the candlelight flickers and throws lacy patterns on the table. I like to use them to dress up a dinner party, but you don't need a fancy occasion to add a little extra sparkle to your evening meal. They make great gifts, too! You can knot this pattern around almost any type of small vessel. From a simple mason jar to handmade ceramics, the choice is yours. Or fill one with fresh water and flowers picked from the yard—it makes a great vase, too.

**FINISHED SIZE**
5½" tall by 8½" around

**KNOTS & TECHNIQUES**
Reverse Lark's Head Knot (RLHK), page 23

Square Knot (SK), page 25

Sinnet of Square Knots, page 27

Alternating Rounds of Square Knots, page 29

Alternating Rows/Rounds of Two (or More) Square Knots, page 29

Horizontal Double Half Hitch (HDHH), page 30

Horizontal Triple Half Hitch (HTHH), page 32 (optional)

**SUPPLIES**
112' worsted weight hemp string

12-ounce jelly jar (5½" tall by 2½" diameter)

Small crochet hook or toothpick (optional)

2½" square of white leather or felt (optional)

Fabric glue (optional)

**CUT LIST**
Two 6' lengths

Twenty 5' lengths

CONTINUED

## KNOTTING

**1** Hold the two 6' strings together and mount the 5' strings onto them one at a time using RLHKs. Fold the mounting cords in half, and group the knots together at the center. [A]

**2** Loop the center of the mounting cords around the lip of the jar and tie an SK where they cross. Take a moment to make sure the cords extending from the SK are all the same length and that the RLHKs are facing out before proceeding. Make sure this loop is very tight around the lip of the jar. It should be removable, but not easily so. [B]

**3** Arrange the RLHKs evenly around the lip of the jar in pairs. Work a round of 3 SKs using all cords, including those used as mounting cords. The sinnet you've worked using the mounting cords should have a total of 4 SKs in it at this point: the one you worked in step 2, plus the 3 you worked in this round.

**4** Work an alternating round of 3 SKs ⅛" below.

**5** Work an alternating round of 8 SKs ⅛" below.

**6** It is easiest to work the remaining rounds and finishing in a seated position, holding the jar between your knees with the bottom facing you. Work 2 alternating rounds of 3 SKs, ⅛" apart.

**7** Work an alternating round of 4–6 SKs, stopping when your knotting reaches the bottom of the jar. [C]

## BASE

You will now work HDHHs in a spiral, gradually removing cords as you work your way to the center. Be sure to work the initial round of the spiral right up against the bottom row of SKs, and each successive round tightly against the previous one. If you leave a large gap between rounds, your spiral may become too small too soon.

**8** Remove the knotting from the jar, and position it so that the bottom (i.e., the side from which the cords extend) is facing you.

**9** Pick up any 2 adjacent cords to use as filler cords in the next step.

**10** Pick up the next cord to the right, and use it to work an HDHH around the filler cords. [D]

**11** Repeat step 10 twice more so that you have worked a total of 3 HDHHs. [E]

**12** Drop a filler cord and let it fall out of the way, down inside the tube of knotting. You will not be knotting this cord any further, so be sure it stays out of the way from now on. Replace the dropped filler cord with the next cord to the right so that you again have 2 filler cords. [F]

**13** Repeat steps 10–12 until you have worked your way around the entire circle. Work your HDHHs so that they sit next to each other, but do not press them together. In addition, if at any point you end up with a significant gap between knots where you can see the filler cords, feel free to substitute an HTHH for an HDHH. This is not strictly necessary, but may improve the look of the bottom of your piece.

CONTINUED

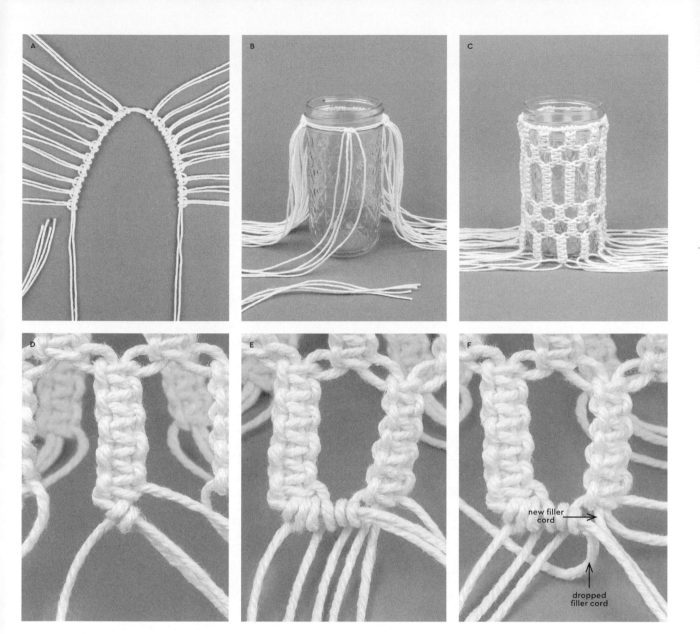

**14** The second and third rounds of the spiral are worked in much the same way as the first, except you will drop and replace filler cords more often. Begin the second round of the spiral by picking up the cord extending from the first HDHH of the first round and using it to work an HDHH around the 2 filler cords. [G]

**15** Drop a filler cord and replace it with the next cord to the right.

**16** Pick up the next cord to the right, and use it to work an HDHH around the filler cords. Repeat so that you have 2 HDHHs in a row. [H]

**17** Repeat steps 15–16 until you have completed the second and third rounds of the spiral.

**18** If the hole at the center of the spiral is now ½" or less, continue on to step 19. If not, continue knotting as you have been until it is.

## FINISHING

**19** Tuck the cords that remain on the outside of the votive through the hole in the center of the spiral, using a small crochet hook or toothpick, if necessary.

**20** Turn the knotting inside out and trim all of the cords to about 1". Press the trimmed ends as flat as possible.

**21** If desired, cut a circle of leather or felt to fit inside the bottom of the votive and conceal the ends, and glue it in place with fabric glue.

**22** Turn the knotting right-side out and place it on the jar.

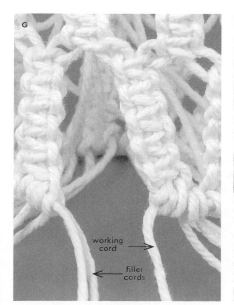

G

working cord

filler cords

H

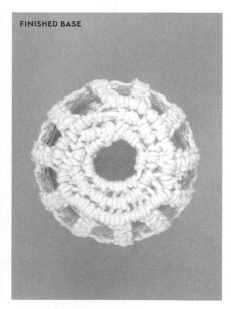

FINISHED BASE

# HOME
# GOODS

Macramé has many lives around the home, from a stylish basket to hold blankets and toys to making the everyday task of sweeping a bit more enjoyable. When we choose to surround ourselves with things that bring us joy, the magic is in the details. This chapter shows you how to craft a handful of projects that will add that special something to any room in the house.

# WRAPPED BROOM HANDLE +

Kara, an assistant of mine, once told me about an argument she and her new husband had over, of all things, shopping for a broom. He didn't understand what was wrong with buying the cheapest one, made of plastic. She wanted something that would bring her joy while doing her chores. Perhaps this project might have helped them reach a compromise! By sprucing up a simple broom with your own knotwork, you can turn a basic household tool into something that adds beauty and pleasure to your chores.

**FINISHED SIZE**
10" long, plus fringe

**KNOTS & TECHNIQUES**
Half Square Knot (HSK), page 24

Mounting with a Half Square Knot (HSK), see page 26

Overhand Knot (OK), page 33

**SUGGESTED SETUP**
There are a few different ways to hold the broom steady while you knot around it. Choose one listed here, or devise your own!

• With the broom standing right-side up, hold the handle steady between your knees as you work the knotting upward, toward yourself.

• Sit in a chair facing a friend. Have them hold the bristled end of the broom steady while you work the knotting around the handle, toward yourself.

• Tie a loop of scrap rope very loosely around the broom handle at its base. Use this loop to hang the broom upside down from a hook, and work the knotting down the handle, toward the floor.

**SUPPLIES**
25' white cotton rope (5mm diameter)

About 3' scrap rope (optional)

Broom

Washi or masking tape (optional)

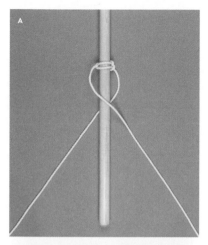

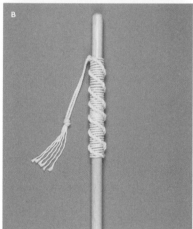

## KNOTTING

1 Mount the 25' rope onto the broom handle about 16" from the end using an HSK. [A] It may be helpful to tape this first knot to the handle to prevent the knotting from sliding around while you work on it.

2 Work 41 additional HSKs, using the broom handle in place of filler cords. Rotate the broom as the knotting spirals, keeping the tension of the knots even as you go.

## FINISHING

3 When you've completed the knotting, slide it into place. It should be about 10" long in all and begin about 4½" from the end of the handle, or at a height at which it rests comfortably between your hands while sweeping.

4 Once your knotting is in place, tie the cords together with an OK, tightening it firmly.

5 Tie a second OK about 8" from the first, making a loop.

6 Unravel the cords create fringe. [B]

# CURTAIN SASH +

This simple sinnet of knotwork brings an effortless touch of handmade warmth to any room. Attach it to the wall with a metal hook and wrap it around nearly any kind of fabric. The drape and texture of a linen or hemp curtain pairs nicely here.

**FINISHED SIZE**
25" long, including fringe, by 1" wide

**KNOTS & TECHNIQUES**
Square Knot (SK), page 25

Mounting with a Square Knot (SK), see page 26

Sinnet of Square Knots, page 27

**SUGGESTED SETUP**
Hook, page 18

**SUPPLIES**
32' white cotton rope (5mm diameter)

1¼" brass ring

**CUT LIST**
One 12' length

Two 10' lengths

## KNOTTING

1 Thread the two 10' ropes through the ring, bringing the ends together so that the center of each one rests on the ring. [A]

2 Bring the center of the 12' rope behind the 4 cords, and mount it onto them using an SK. [B]

3 Work 15 SKs below the first. [C]

4 Pick up 1 filler cord in each hand and bring them out to the sides, behind the working cords. Use these as working cords in the remaining knotting. [D]

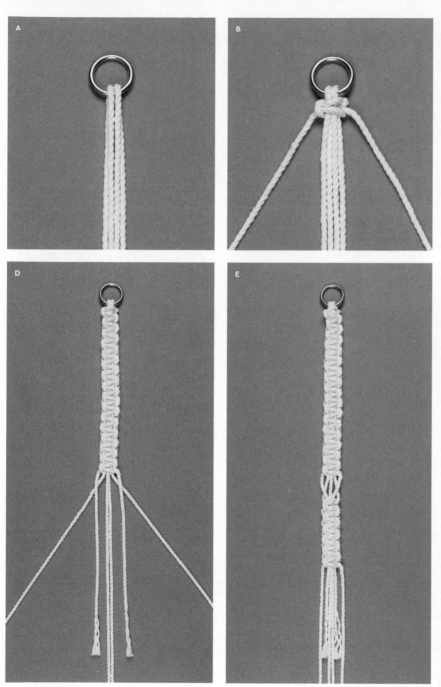

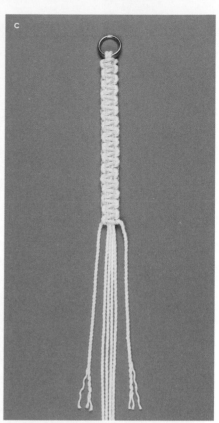

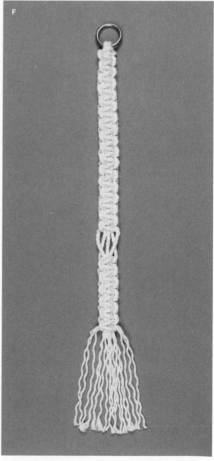

**5** Starting 2" below the knots you've already made, work 6 SKs. [E]

## FINISHING

**6** Trim all cords 6" below the knotting and unravel them. [F]

# MARKET BAG ++

A versatile companion, this bag is as equally suited for a flower-foraging expedition, with branches and blossoms peeking out of the top and sides, as it is a trip to the farmers' market to be filled with all the fixings for an inspired meal. Or throw it on with a special outfit and fancy shoes on your way to an art opening.

**FINISHED SIZE**
40" long, including strap and fringe, by 13" wide

**KNOTS & TECHNIQUES**
Reverse Lark's Head Knot (RLHK), page 23

Square Knot (SK), page 25

Sinnet of Square Knots (SKs), page 27

Alternating Rounds of Square Knots, page 29

Alternating Rows/Rounds of Two (or More) Square Knots, page 29

**SUGGESTED SETUP**
Hook, page 18

**SUPPLIES**
422' jute rope (¼" diameter)

**CUT LIST**
One 30' length

Thirty-two 12' lengths

One 8' length

CONTINUED

## STRAP

1  Fold the 30' rope in half and cross its cords 21" inches from the center to make a loop. This loop will form the opening at the top of the bag.

2  Fold the 8' rope in half over the *X* you made with the 30' rope. [A] Take a moment to make sure that the *X* is still 21" from the center of the loop before proceeding. [B]

3  Using the 2 longer cords as working cords and the 2 shorter cords as filler, work a 31"-long sinnet of SKs.

4  Attach the strap to the opposite side of the loop by bringing the filler cords in front of the looped cord and the working cords behind it, and then working an SK. You can now hang the strap from a hook to work the rest of the knotting. [C]

5  Using RLHKs, mount a 12' rope onto the loop on either side of the SK you just worked. You now have 8 cords hanging down from your work. [D]

6  Using the first and eighth cords as working cords, work a sinnet of 4 SKs around the 6 cords between them, keeping those extending from the strap toward the back of the group of filler cords. Trim the ends of the 4 cords used to make the strap as close to the lowest SK as possible, being careful not to trim the 4 cords you just mounted onto the loop.

7  Mount a 12' rope onto the loop on either side of the other end of the strap. Use these newly mounted cords to work a sinnet of 4 SKs.

## BODY

8  Mount the 28 remaining 12' ropes onto the loop using RLHKs, spacing them evenly in pairs and being sure to mount 14 ropes on each side of the bag.

9  Work a sinnet of 2 SKs with each group of 4 cords mounted in the previous step. [E]

10  Work 2 alternating rounds of 2 SKs.

11  Work an alternating round of 6 SKs.

12  Crisscross the sinnets of the previous round left over right and work an alternating round of 2 SKs. [F]

13  Work another 4 alternating rounds of 2 SKs.

## JOINING THE BOTTOM

14  Next, you will knot the bottom of the bag together. First, using the leftmost 4 cords (i.e., the leftmost 2 cords from the side of the bag facing you and the leftmost 2 from the side facing away), work a sinnet of 2 SKs. Repeat on the right side. These SKs should face left and right respectively, not forward. In other words, with the bag flattened, you should be looking at these knots in profile.

15  Flatten the bag. Pick up 4 cords next to one of the sinnets worked in the previous step, along with the 4 cords directly behind them. Take a moment to make sure that the cords in back are not twisted. Then work a sinnet of 2 SKs using the first and fourth cords of those in front as working cords and the remaining 6 cords (i.e., the 2 cords between the working cords and the 4 cords coming from the back of the bag) as filler. Repeat with the remaining cords, closing the bottom of the bag. This row, like those above it, is alternating. Make sure that your knots lie between those above them and that you have used every single cord.

## FINISHING

16  Trim all cords to 6" and unravel them. [G]

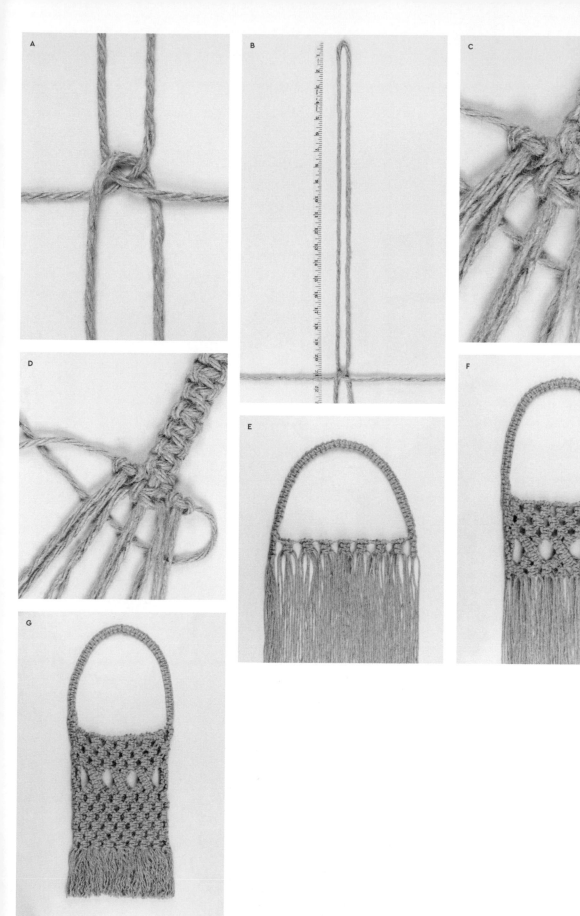

# PILLOW COVER ++

Cozy up on the couch with your new favorite pillow—or two or three! This basic pattern can easily be varied once you get the hang of it. Make a few in different colors or try incorporating extra fringe. You could replace the geometric knotting pattern with one of your own design, or even just turn it over to show the back for a more graphic look. Or simply use brightly colored pillow inserts to make the texture and pattern of the knots really pop.

**FINISHED SIZE**
22" square (to fit a 22–24" square pillow insert)

**KNOTS & TECHNIQUES**
Lark's Head Knot (LHK), page 23

Square Knot (SK), page 25

Alternating Square Knots (ASK), page 28

Alternating Rows of Square Knots, page 29

Horizontal Double Half Hitch (HDHH), page 30

Overhand Knot (OK), page 33

**SUGGESTED SETUP**
Supported Dowel or Hanging Dowel, page 18*

**SUPPLIES**
831' white cotton rope (5mm diameter)

Washi or masking tape

10–12mm crochet hook

22–24" square pillow insert

**CUT LIST**
Thirty-four 24' lengths

One 10' length

One 5' length

*For this project it is important to use a dowel with a diameter of at least 1", as the size of the dowel determines the length of the fringe along the top edge.

CONTINUED

## PREPARATION

1 Tape off a 24" workspace on the dowel.

2 Mount all of the 24' ropes onto the dowel using LHKs, and space them evenly across your workspace.

## FLAP

3 Work 5 rows of ASKs. [A] Throughout this project, each row of ASKs should take up about ⅝" of vertical space, meaning all five rows so far should measure about 3¼" from top to bottom. Take a moment to measure the height of the 5 rows you just worked. If your measurement is more than ½" off, I strongly recommend taking a few minutes to adjust your knotting. If you don't, you may end up with a much different-sized piece, and could even run out of rope before finishing.

4 Using the 5' rope as the filler cord, work a row of HDHHs from left to right, leaving a tail at either end of the filler cord of about 18". Be sure to tighten each HDHH just enough to keep it positioned directly below the SK above it. If your knots aren't tight enough, then this row will end up wider than the ASKs above it. If they are too tight, the row will be too narrow. [B]

## FRONT

5 Work 5 rows of ASKs. [C]

6 Use the following row-by-row instructions along with the bottom photo on the facing page to complete the geometric pattern.

Row 1: Skip the first 2 cords. [Repeat 5 times: Work an SK, skip 8 cords.] Work an SK, then skip the last 2 cords.

Row 2: Work an SK. [Repeat 5 times: Work an SK, skip 4 cords, work an SK.] Work an SK.

Row 3: Skip the first 6 cords. [Repeat 5 times: Work 2 SKs, skip 4 cords.] Skip the last 2 cords.

Row 4: Skip the first 8 cords. [Repeat 5 times: Work an SK, skip 8 cords.]

Row 5: Repeat Row 3.

Row 6: Repeat Row 2.

Row 7: Repeat Row 1.

Row 8: Skip the first 4 cords. [Repeat 2 times: Work an SK, skip 4 cords, work an SK.] Skip 4 cords, work an SK, then skip 4 cords. [Repeat 2 times: Work an SK, skip 4 cords, work an SK.] Skip the last 4 cords.

Row 9: Repeat Row 3.

Row 10: Work an SK, skip 4 cords, work an SK, skip 8 cords. [Repeat 3 times: Work an SK, skip 4 cords]. Work an SK, skip 8 cords, work an SK, skip 4 cords, then work an SK. [D]

Row 11: Skip the first 2 cords. [Repeat 3 times: Work an SK, skip 4 cords.] Work an SK, then skip 8 cords. [Repeat 3 times: Work an SK, skip 4 cords.] Work an SK, then skip the last 2 cords.

Row 12: Repeat Row 8.

CONTINUED

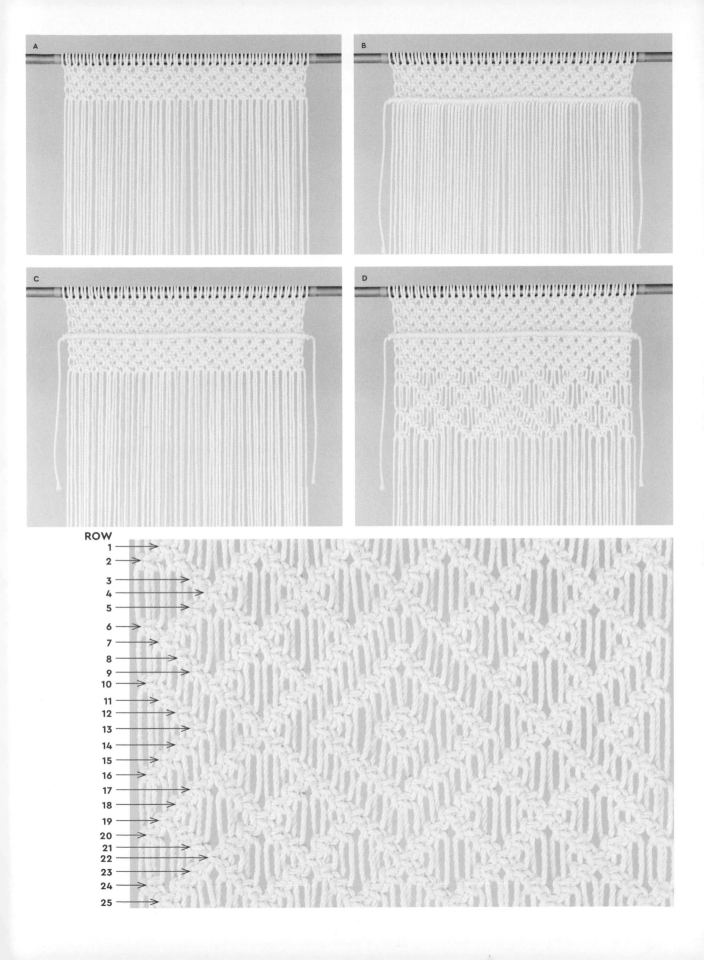

A

B

C

D

ROW

1
2
3
4
5
6
7
8
9
10
11
12
13
14
15
16
17
18
19
20
21
22
23
24
25

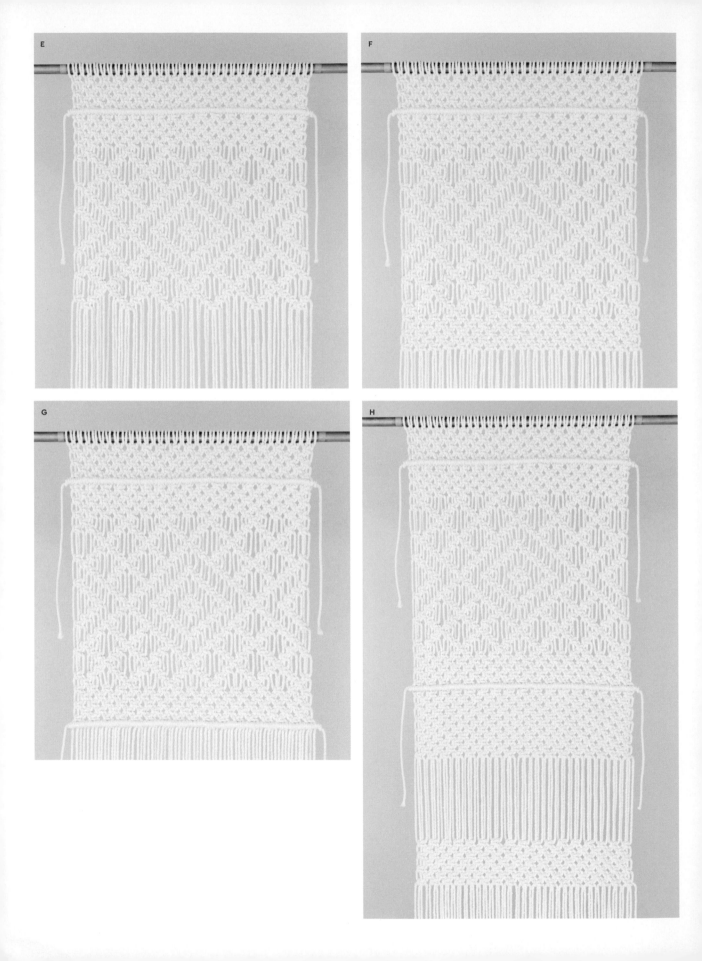

Row 13: This is the central row of the pattern. Skip the first 6 cords. [Repeat 3 times: Work an SK, skip 4 cords.] Work an SK. [Repeat 3 times: Work an SK, skip 4 cords.] Work an SK, then skip the last 6 cords.

Because the diamond pattern is vertically symmetrical, you can now simply work the first 12 rows in reverse to complete it.

Row 14: Repeat Row 12

Row 15: Repeat Row 11

Row 16: Repeat Row 10

Row 17: Repeat Row 9

Row 18: Repeat Row 8

Row 19: Repeat Row 7

Row 20: Repeat Row 6

Row 21: Repeat Row 5

Row 22: Repeat Row 4

Row 23: Repeat Row 3

Row 24: Repeat Row 2

Row 25: Repeat Row 1 [E]

7 Work 5 rows of ASKs. [F]

8 Using the 10' rope as the filler cord, work a row of HDHHs, leaving a tail of about 48" at either end of the filler cord. [G]

## BACK

9 Work 11 rows of ASKs.

10 Starting 8" below, work 7 rows of ASKs. [H]

CONTINUED

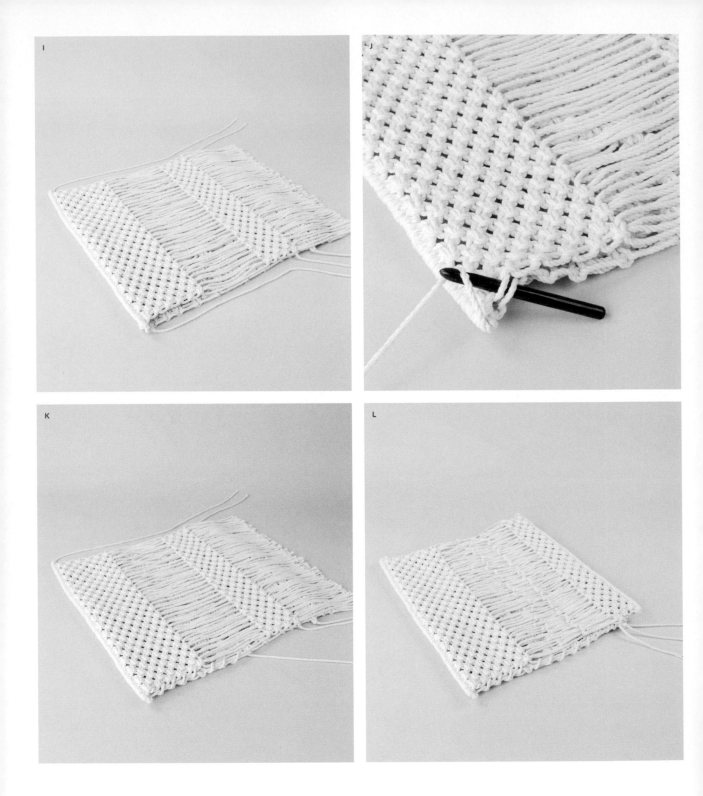

## FINISHING

**11** Set aside the rightmost cord along the bottom edge, and trim the rest to 8". *Do not trim the tails at the ends of the HDHH rows.*

**12** Working outward from the center, remove the pillow cover from the dowel by cutting each rope at the center of its LHK. (See Welcome Home Accent Rug, step 8, page 174.)

**13** Fold the rectangle at the second row of HDHHs and lay it flat with the back facing you. [I]

**14** At one of the corners, just below the HDHHs, poke the crochet hook up through both layers of knotting (making sure they are lined up) and pull the filler cord down through both layers. [J]

**15** Repeat, wrapping the cord around the edge and between each row of SKs until you reach the end of the knotting on the shorter layer. Secure the cord to a neighbor using 2 OKs. The exact number of "stitches" you make is less important here than making sure the sides line up properly. [K]

**16** Repeat steps 14–15 on the other side.

**17** Fold down the flap, and use the same method to stitch along its short sides as well. [L]

**18** Place the pillow insert inside. Use the remaining long cord to stitch the back and flap together. Once finished, secure the cord you stitched with to an adjacent cord using 2 OKs.

**19** Trim any long cords that remain to match the length of the fringe.

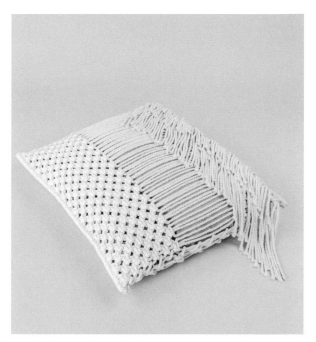

# BASKET +++

In my house, there are baskets everywhere. They greet me at the front door filled with umbrellas, hats, and gloves. There is one in the living room nestling folded blankets. I have a basket in the bathroom with a reserve of towels at the ready, and two in the bedroom for everyday wear and more delicate laundry.

I designed this basket with versatility in mind. The durability of its material means it could house a plant pot or even withstand life outdoors! If made instead out of thick cotton, it could be a laundry basket or a receptacle for toys and other items you might like to tuck away quickly out of sight.

This pattern includes two knotting options for the body of the basket. When you get to that portion of the method, simply choose either Body A (pictured opposite, right) or Body B (pictured opposite, left) and follow the instructions.

**FINISHED SIZE**
22" tall by 44" around

**KNOTS & TECHNIQUES**
Reverse Lark's Head Knot (RLHK), page 23

Square Knot (SK), page 25

Sinnet of Square Knots, page 27

Alternating Square Knot (ASK), page 28

Alternating Rounds of Square Knots, page 29

Alternating Rows/Rounds of Two (or More) Square Knots, page 29

Horizontal Double Half Hitch (HDHH), page 30

**SUGGESTED SETUPS**
Supported Dowel or Hanging Dowel, page 18

**SUPPLIES**
586' polypropylene jute rope (⅜" diameter)

Gardening gloves

Washi or masking tape

2 S-hooks

12" square of leather or felt

Fabric glue (optional)

**CUT LIST**
One 34' length

Twenty-three 24' lengths

CONTINUED

A note on the material: Polypropylene rope is highly durable but takes a bit of extra muscle to knot, and it also tends to shed. So throw on some comfy work clothes and a pair of gardening gloves, and plan to take some breaks to stretch as you work.

In addition, the technique used to form the bottom of the basket can be challenging at first, especially when using this material. If you haven't tried it before, you may find it helpful to make the Wrapped Votive (page 209) first, a project that includes the same technique but is made of a softer, more malleable material.

## TOP

1 Fold the 34' rope in half, and mark the center with a piece of tape. At the center of the rope, make a doubled-over loop with a circumference of 44". If desired, tape the crossed cords lightly onto the taped center point to maintain the loop's size during the next step. [A]

2 Mount one of the 24' lengths onto the loop at the point where the ends cross using an RLHK. [B]

3 Using the ends of the looped rope as working cords, work an SK. [C]

4 Mount the remaining twenty-two 24' lengths onto the loop using RLHKs, and space them evenly. You can now hang your project up to work the knotting by placing the S-hooks opposite each other on the loop and then hanging them from the dowel.

## BODY

5 Work either Body A or Body B.

  i. Body A

  Rounds 1–14: Work 14 rounds of ASKs.

  ii. Body B

  Rounds 1–6: Work 6 rounds of ASKs.

  Round 7: Work 1 alternating round of 3 SKs.

  Rounds 8–15: Work 8 rounds of ASKs.

## BASE

You will now work HDHHs in a spiral, gradually removing cords as you work your way to the center. Be sure to tighten these knots as thoroughly as possible to ensure that the bottom of your basket is durable. If you plan to place heavy items inside, you may also wish to place a dot of fabric glue inside these knots to prevent the bottom of the basket from stretching out over time.

6 Remove the basket from the S-hooks, and invert it so that the bottom is facing you.

7 Pick up any two adjacent cords to use as filler cords in the next step.

8 Pick up the next cord to the right and use it to work an HDHH around the filler cords. [D]

9 Repeat step 8 three times so that you have worked a total of 4 HDHHs. [E]

10 Drop a filler cord and place it out of the way inside the basket. You will not be knotting this cord any further, so be sure it stays out of the way from now on. You may want to mark it with a piece of tape to avoid accidentally knotting it later. Replace the dropped filler cord with the next cord to the right so that you again have two filler cords. [F]

CONTINUED

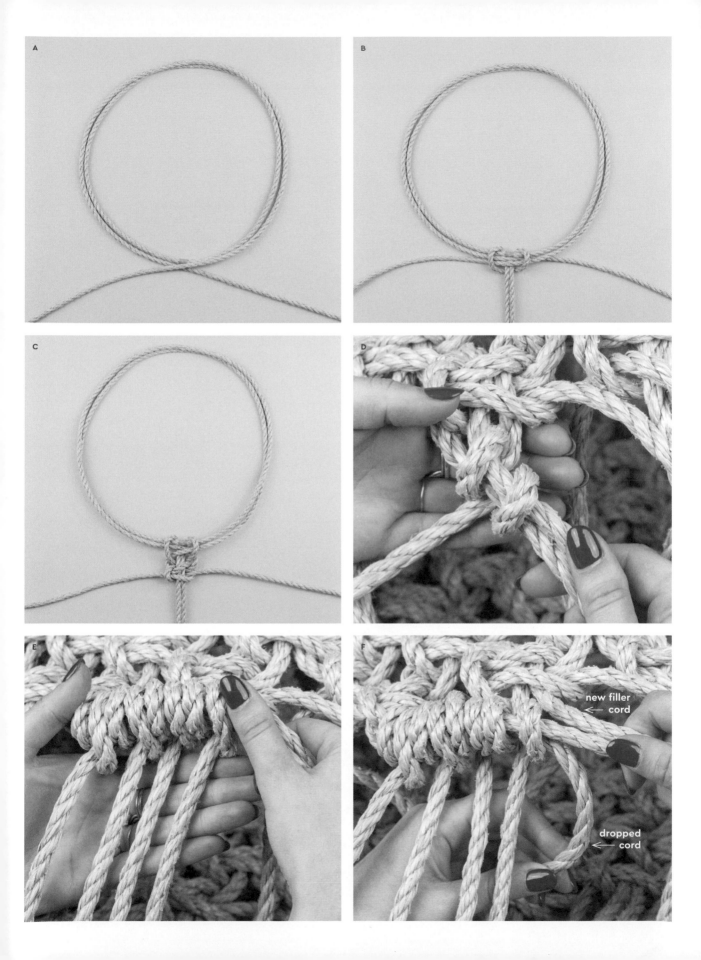

A

B

C

D

E

F

new filler
cord

dropped
cord

**11** Repeat steps 8–10 until you have worked your way around the basket. [G] When you reach the beginning of the second round, simply continue on to the working cord of the first HDHH of the first round. [H]

**12** For the third round of the spiral, you will decrease the number of working cords more quickly than you did in the first 2 rounds. For this round, after every 3 HDHHs drop a filler cord into the basket and replace it with the next cord to the right.

**13** Work your way around the spiral for a fourth time; this time drop and replace a filler cord after every 2 HDHHs. If you reach the center of the spiral before you finish this round, stop knotting and continue on to Finishing.

**14** If possible, continue spiraling around a fifth time, dropping a filler cord and replacing it after every HDHH. If you reach the center of the spiral before you finish this round, stop knotting and continue on to Finishing.

## FINISHING

**15** Pull the remaining working cords through the center of the spiral to the inside of the basket.

**16** Trim all of the loose cords inside the basket to about 5" and press them as flat as possible.

**17** Measure the diameter of the inside of the base of the basket, and cut out a circle of leather or felt of this size.

**18** Lay the circle of leather or felt on top of the loose ends at the bottom of the basket, gluing it in place if desired.

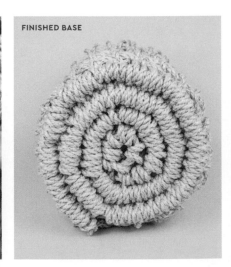

FINISHED BASE

# RESOURCES

When I began my macramé journey, good materials were nearly impossible to find. I saw a need for high-quality rope, beads, dowels, and more, and now you can find most of what you need to make the projects in this book at modernmacrame.com. For everything else I have made a list of my favorite sources.

## FRAMES AND ACCESSORIES

**Beckel Canvas Products**
beckelcanvas.com
Wall tent frame

**Byer of Maine**
byerofmaine.com
Sling chair, daybed frame

**Color Cord Company**
colorcord.com
Pendant light cord

**Rainbow Lampshade Shop**
rainbowlampshadeshop.com
Lampshade spiders

**Soñadora Studio**
etsy.com/shop/SonadoraStudio
Steel-frame hoop chair

## FOR STYLING

**Block Shop**
blockshoptextiles.com
Block-printed textiles

**Bobbie Specker**
bobbiespeckerceramics.com
Ceramic planters and vases

**Collectivo**
ourcollectivo.com
Handcrafted textiles

**The Granite**
workshop-thegranite.com
Ceramic vases

**Martina Thornhill**
martinathornhill.com
Ceramics and dishes

**Spartan Shop**
spartan-shop.com
Inspired and elegant goods
for the home

# GLOSSARY

**Alternating** Horizontally offset as compared to the previous row. An alternating knot lies halfway between the two knots above it because it is made with half of the cords extending from each. (See photo on page 28.)

**Column** Two or more knots worked in sequence.

**Contrast Color (CC)** The secondary color in a project containing two colors; the second most prevalent color in a project containing more than two colors.

**Contrast Color Two (CC2)** The secondary contrast color in a project containing three or more colors.

**Cord** Either side of a rope that has been folded in half. A single rope, once folded, yields two cords, with which or around which knotting can be formed. In other words, the term "ropes" refers to entire cut lengths. "Cords" are what are actually used to form knots.

**Filler cord(s)** Cord(s) around which knots are formed by working cords.

**Held double** Used two at a time, so two cords serve as one. (See photo B on page 100.)

**In sequence** Using the same cords as the knot above, and therefore directly beneath it. Knots worked in sequence may or may not have vertical space between them. (See page 27.)

**Main Color (MC)** The most prevalent color in a project containing more than one color.

**Mount** To incorporate a new rope into a project using a knot. Ropes may be mounted onto other ropes already in use, a mounting cord, or a solid object like a dowel or hoop.

**Mounting cord** Rope onto which other ropes are mounted.

**Netting** Knotting pattern using alternating knots to create mesh. (See page 28.)

**Plied** Rope made from two or more strands twisted together.

**Rope** An entire cut length of any type of knotting material. Once folded in half, a rope is said to have two cords.

**Round** Horizontal sequence of knots across all cords worked in a circle. A piece with a circular or tubular shape is said to be worked in rounds as opposed to rows.

**Row** Horizontal sequence of knots across all cords.

**Sinnet** Column of directly adjacent knots of the same type. (See top photo on page 27.)

**Swatch** Small sample of knotted material. (See page 34.)

**Working cord** Cord used to form knots.

# ACKNOWLEDGMENTS

This book would not be here if it weren't for my mom, who taught me macramé in her kitchen and who helped with the writing for the proposal of this book. It also wouldn't be here (and I also wouldn't be here . . .) if it were not for my dad, who always inspired me to be the best version of myself I can be, and who has fantastic taste in design.

To my grandmother, who passed away in April 2017 while I was finishing this manuscript. She inspired my deep appreciation of food and travel, and though we didn't get to spend nearly enough time together, my dream is to cross off the rest of her bucket list, by eating and sailing and experiencing the beauty of the world.

This book would probably never have come to be if not for Jen Jones, who put the idea into my head back in 2014, while on my first-ever macramé tour in California, that I could be the one to make this macramé book.

One million THANK-YOUs to my ALL-WOMAN team who made this book possible: Anne Parker for the thoughtful eye offered toward so many parts of making this book happen. Your styling skills, editing prowess, and producing/planning were essential, plus you make a mean margarita. Nicole Franzen for taking such incredible photographs, and for being flexible and open to being a part of this. I always admired your work, and now I am so grateful to call you a collaborator and friend. Shannon Wolf, for taking the DIY photos and staying on top of making sure

the macramé business keeps on growing and flowing. You are a multitasking master. Johanna Kunin, without whom this book would be chicken scratch. Your attention to detail, thoughtful writing, and dedication to the project means everything to me. Plus, your dad jokes are the best. Anja Charbonneau, for helping us in the initial stages. Your experience made the process so much clearer and more refined. Rachel Grimes, for sharing your authentic self, for putting love into your work, and for your constant expression of gratitude. Your kind and caring words are often my favorite part of my day. Karen Cygnarowicz, for editing, rope cutting, and being a wonderful part of the team. Your hard work is just another kind of poetry. Martina Thornhill, for getting things organized, loaning us amazing ceramics, and generally being awesome. Elizabeth Artis, for your plant magic and dear friendship. Kara Jean Sonwell, for jumping in and being helpful with a smile always. Corbin Lamont, for designing our graphic charts. Deena Prichep, for help with the proposal. Kristina Morris, for designing the visual proposal.

To my amazing agent, Betsy Amster, whose support and guidance pushed me to think big and to be clear and precise.

To all the people at Ten Speed: Ashley Lima, Mari Gill, Natalie Mulford, Windy Dorresteyn, and Daniel Myers, who deeply believe in this project and are lovingly working to make it a huge success. Thank you, especially, to my editor Kaitlin Ketchum, who made the process of pulling together this book as dreamy as such a giant undertaking can be. I knew from our first phone call that you and Ten Speed were the right fit!

To my pattern testers: Adam Thompson, Ashley Marcu, Ashley Mudra, James Evans Harvey, Kady Monroe-Tracey, Kara Jean Sonwell, Karen Cygnarowicz, Rachel Grimes, Sara Bergman, and Sarah Fennell. THANK YOU for lending your time and offering thoughtful feedback.

This book would be nothing if not for the incredible hospitality of all the people who welcomed us into their homes to shoot the projects: Chloe Fields, Liz Kamarul, Jessica Helgerson, Anne Parker, and Jenna Wilson in Portland, Oregon; Laura and Jason O'Dell, Mariah O'Brien, Caroline and Jayden Lee, Lisa Cole, Malia and Jess Bianchi-Mau, and Jennifer Siegal in Los Angeles, California; Sohail Zandi and Sara Elbert, and Kelli Cain and Brian Crabtree in upstate New York; and Kenn Husted, Rikke Graff Juel, Jonas and Justine Djernes-Bell, Peter Amby, and my dreamy loves Natasha and Dan Husted in Copenhagen, Denmark.

To the amazing designers and companies who lent us beautiful things to shoot: Blockshop, Martina Thornhill, Neapolitan Shop, Schoolhouse Electric, Bobbie Specker, The Granite, Spartan Shop, and Mazama Wares.

To Rudolf and Gina, for hosting us in Los Angeles. To Lauren and Nialls Fallon, for being the best New York City hosts ever. To Chandler and Josh Busby in Haiti. To Anna Korte, for being a test subject when the book was just a baby idea. To Leela Cyd, for the intro to Betsy, taking some beautiful photos to get it all started, and lending your ear and support. To my sister, Eleena, for the catch-ups over wine.

To the macramé artists who came before me, and who are making incredible work now as well. I wanted to feature you all here, but I will have to wait until the next book to do that.

To my sweetheart, Adam Porterfield, for supporting me throughout this process with cocktails, healthful dinners, drawn baths, and foot massages. Thank you for loving me despite my constant travel, long hours, dedication to this project, and all of my crazy ideas. May we continue to expand and grow together. I love you with all my heart. We are ever knotted together with ribbons of light.

AND TO YOU! Who will bring this book into your homes, make beautiful things from it to adorn your space, celebrate momentous occasions, and gather together, connecting over craft.

# ABOUT THE AUTHOR

Emily Katz is an artist, world traveler, teacher, interior designer, creative consultant, public speaker, social-media phenomenon, and the owner of Modern Macramé.

Emily has taught macramé to thousands worldwide through private lessons and team-building workshops, from L.A. to Tokyo to Copenhagen. Her creativity doesn't stop there; she has designed restaurant interiors and residences inspired by her travels, as well as large-scale custom macramé installations for clients such as Ralph Lauren, Microsoft, and Nordstrom.

Named as the "Queen of Macramé" by the *Guardian UK*, her work has also been featured in the *Los Angeles Times*, *Elle Japan*, BuzzFeed, and more. As a self-made entrepreneur for over fifteen years, Emily employs an all-woman team of creatives at her studio, which serves as a production center, showroom, office, and event space.

Emily lives in Portland, Oregon, with her partner, Adam, their dog, Donut, and cat, Cowbear.

*Modern Macramé* is her first book.

Instagram: @emily_katz and @modernmacrame

modernmacrame.com

emilykatz.com

# INDEX

Library of Congress Cataloging-in-Publication Data
is on file with the publisher.

Hardcover ISBN: 978-0-399-57957-8
eBook ISBN: 978-0-399-57958-5

Printed in China

Design by Ashley Lima
Prop styling by Anne Parker
Pattern text by Johanna Kunin
Tutorial photographs by Shannon Wolf

10 9 8 7 6 5 4 3 2 1

First Edition

Library of Congress Cataloging-in-Publication Data
is on file with the publisher.

Hardcover ISBN: 978-0-399-57957-8
eBook ISBN: 978-0-399-57958-5

Printed in China

Design by Ashley Lima
Prop styling by Anne Parker
Pattern text by Johanna Kunin
Tutorial photographs by Shannon Wolf

10 9 8 7 6 5 4 3 2 1

First Edition